Cars I Could've,
Should've, Kept

Cars I Could've, Should've, Kept

Memoir of a Life Restoring Classic Sports Cars

JACKSON BROOKS

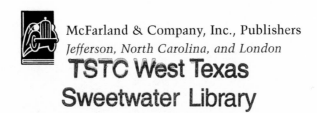

McFarland & Company, Inc., Publishers
Jefferson, North Carolina, and London

Estimated values from *Sports Car Market Price Guide* used by permission.

LIBRARY OF CONGRESS CATALOGUING-IN-PUBLICATION DATA

Brooks, Jackson, 1922–
    Cars I could've, should've, kept : memoir of a life restoring classic sports cars / Jackson Brooks.
      p.   cm.
    Includes index.

    ISBN-13: 978-0-7864-2810-6
    softcover : 50# alkaline paper ∞

    1. Brooks, Jackson, 1922– . 2. Sports cars—Collectors and collecting—Biography. 3. Sports cars—Conservation and restoration—Case studies 4. Automobile engineers—United States—Biography. I. Title.
TL140.B76A3 2007
629.222'1—dc22
[B]   2007003591

British Library cataloguing data are available

On the cover: *top* Packard Individual Dietrich Victoria, No. 904-95; *bottom* 1930 Alfa Romeo 6C-1750 Zagato

Manufactured in the United States of America

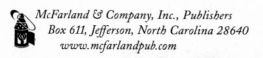
McFarland & Company, Inc., Publishers
Box 611, Jefferson, North Carolina 28640
www.mcfarlandpub.com

DEDICATED TO

Ron Kerr and Loran Swanson, two very talented men who did most of
the work. Gene Rouse, who was with me in the beginning. John O'Donnell,
who usually had parts. Keith Hellon, who inspired me. Arlen Goodwine,
the brilliant one. Phil Reilly and his elves that could fix things we couldn't.
Phil Hill, who raced my Alfa. John deBoer, who tracks Alfas. Peter
Giddings, Simon Moore and all the other good Englishmen that love
cars and answered my letters. Ray Middleton, who will never sell his Alvis.
Mark Clayton, who restores 100-point Classic Cars. Jerry Munson, who
left us too soon. Gordon Barrett, who hauled his 8C Alfa 200 miles out
of his way to surprise an old man. My wife and four kids, Robin, Barbara,
Jennifr and Brian, who said I should do this someday. And especially to
Tom Haynie, my son-in-law who prodded me to do it *now*.

...And to all the others whose tire-tracks I crossed.

Contents

Preface

To succeed as an artist requires at least four things: talent, training, a good work ethic and passion. One might become just an OK artist without all four, but talent and a passion for what you're doing are essential. The more I studied art as a young man, the more I realized my talent was too small, and when you realize you're short on talent it sort of pours cold water on your passion. Besides, fine artists were starving during the Depression. I didn't want to starve or be just a middling artist. I had learned enough to recognize good art when I saw it, and to know that mine was not good. So I turned to commercial art, entering the neon sign business in 1945, and have never regretted my decision.

By 1962 I was forty years old, married with four kids ranging from eighteen to ten years old, and I was still building my business. When you are a small business entrepreneur, you're always at risk. It's a constant battle but it can also be very fulfilling. I had become a pretty good businessman, but I worked too much and I needed a hobby. I had liked cars as a kid even though my dad seldom owned one. When I could finally afford to buy my first car, at age thirteen, with money earned delivering two paper routes, it was a $10 Model T Ford, and then I bought a $75 air-cooled Franklin. I bought the Franklin because, being an off-breed make, it was cheaper than a Ford or a Chevrolet and to me, a lot more interesting. I could overhaul one cylinder at a time, which I did—pretty often, because I learned to run it on kerosene. I would put gasoline in the vacuum tank to start the car, then, with a petcock valve, I would switch it to kerosene in the main gas tank. Gasoline was ten cents a gallon and kerosene was only five cents. With its 4.5:1 compression ratio the Franklin ran great on

1

the kerosene once the engine was hot, but I had to clean the carbon off the valves and piston tops pretty regularly. By the time I could afford my first new car I had owned three Auburns, a supercharged Cord phaeton, a Chrysler Town and Country convertible and a few others not worth mentioning. I had just enough artistic talent to appreciate good design, and the neon sign business had taught me to appreciate good craftsmanship.

Watching the *Denver Post* classified ads for something interesting, I found a restored 1929 Chrysler Le Mans Series 75 rumble seat roadster with wire wheels and twin side-mounted spares for $1,000 in Colorado Springs. I drove down to see it, and having no idea of its worth, I made a standing offer of $500. The owner was in the military and was being shipped overseas, and when he got no better offer he accepted mine. I had a lot of fun driving that car, with my wife up front and a couple of the kids in the rumble seat. I also liked to tinker with it, doing the routine maintenance in my garage. The only thing I made for the Chrysler was a chrome-plated bronze casting of a hubcap to replace one that was missing.

I enjoy reading about anything I am interested in, so I subscribed to John Bond's *Road & Track* magazine and began looking for books about interesting cars. Today there are thousands of car books, but almost none were published in America at that time. L. Scott Bailey began publishing *Automobile Quarterly* in 1962 and I was a subscriber for the next forty years. Initially, Ken Purdy, Ralph Stein, John Bond, Denise McCluggage and others were contributing authors. I found that I took great pleasure in reading about the fascinating, talented people who designed, built and raced cars. To me the people were at least as interesting as the cars. Ken Purdy wrote articles about the great cars for *Playboy* magazine, and it was amazing how many men convinced their wives that his articles were the only reason they were subscribers. He eventually compiled those into a book. Ralph Stein was a well-known New England cartoonist who loved cars. He bought, sold and traded them almost as often as I would a few years later. He wrote his first book, *Treasury of the Automobile*, in 1961. Denise McCluggage was the only successful American woman racecar driver that I knew of at that time. She also wrote well, from first-hand knowledge, and still does forty years later.

For Christmas 1962, my wife, Jackie, found a book published in England titled *Cars of the Connoisseurs* by J. R. Buckley. His book was a revelation to me. Edwardian and Vintage automobiles and sports-racing cars were extremely popular in England. Moreover, there were many club events, shows, hill-climbs and races for old cars in England. By comparison, there were very few car activities in America in the early sixties, and those few were mostly in New England, the Chicago region and

California. The interest in foreign sports cars began when returning American GIs, who had seen them in England and Europe, wanted them. Wealthy young men like Briggs Cunningham, the Collier brothers and a few others who could afford the more expensive sports cars started the Sports Car Club of America by having races on the Colliers' family estate. There were a few sports car enthusiasts in Colorado Springs, Denver and Boulder, but in Fort Collins, which was then just a small college town of 30,000 people, 65 miles north of Denver, I was alone, in a comparative automobile wilderness.

After reading about all the wonderful cars, especially those in Buckley's book, I decided that the one I would most like to own was an 8C-2.3 liter supercharged Alfa Romeo. Only 188 were built from 1931 to 1934. Not surprisingly, I had never seen an Alfa Romeo and had no idea where to begin looking for one. Through *Road & Track*, though, I discovered there was an Alfa Romeo club. I became a member to get their newsletter, edited and printed by Pat Braden whenever the spirit moved him. Besides articles, the newsletter contained an occasional ad for a vintage Alfa, usually a non-runner. Most of the few 8C Alfas in America were in the northeastern region where the interest in such cars began.

I decided to sell my Chrysler to buy an Alfa if one came along I could afford. I sold the Chrysler for $1,800, over three times what I had paid for it. That convinced me that perhaps this car hobby might disprove the old adage that "you can't have your cake and eat it too." On the rare occasion when an 8C Alfa Spider (roadster) was advertised, even then a good running 8C Spider cost from $5,000 to $10,000. That was equivalent to $35,000 to $70,000 in today's play-money, which was far more than I could afford. Had I been clairvoyant, I would have sold my neon sign company and bought every one I could lay my hands on. But I wasn't.

But this book is not just about Alfa Romeos or an automobile collection. Rather, it is a trip through my memory and photo album with me telling about the many cars that I bought, restored and drove over the ensuing decades. It also includes photos of cars that I took in trade, or bought and kept for a while, just to have the experience of driving them, then selling them to invest in another car. The photos are not professional—almost all of them were taken by me, and many have been given away to those who bought my cars. Had I known how important and valuable some of these cars would become, I would have hired a professional photographer for every one. Their aggregate value at today's prices would be from thirty to forty million dollars!

Now in my twilight years, I sometimes wonder what it was that led me straight to the very best of the cars that are almost priceless today, and

I now know I could not have chosen the cars that I did without that small spark of talent and artistic taste. I was first attracted by a car's looks, then learned to appreciate equally the mechanical design that was no less artistic on the really great cars. I now marvel at the energy and passion I brought to this car hobby.

I also marvel at how I was able to devote so much time and energy to the hobby without neglecting my family or business, but I neglected neither. My experience, for the next thirty years, was so unique that many people told me I should write a book about my cars. I have done so. It is written largely from memory, so perhaps the inevitable errors and omissions can be excused. Keep in mind that I was never a collector. For me it was meeting the challenge of doing the restoration, sometimes to save the car from oblivion, that gave me so much satisfaction. It was another way I could express my small artistic talent and creativity. A brief story about each car may help the reader understand what I found so fascinating about some of the very rare cars that were made before they became almost too precious to drive.

1

The 8C-2.3 Alfa Romeo

After selling the Chrysler and putting the money aside, in 1965 I finally saw an ad for an 8C-2.3 Alfa Romeo Berlinetta (2-door coupe) for $2,500 in Wayland, a village in upstate New York, not far from Watkins Glen. The ad said it "could be driven anywhere." Coincidentally, about that time I was asked to teach a seminar in Atlanta for one of our electric sign industry associations. I refused a fee, but they offered an all expense-paid trip to Bermuda for my wife and me. I asked if instead of Bermuda they would pay our air fare for a trip to New York, so I could go look at this Alfa Romeo. Jackie wasn't too happy to trade a trip to Bermuda for a trip to Wayland, New York. Needless to say, it took all my skills as a salesman to convince Jackie this would be just as much fun as Bermuda. So we flew to Newark, New Jersey. Upon landing, Jackie mentioned Bermuda again and I had to admit that Newark didn't look or smell much like a vacation-land.

I rented a car, and we drove first to Westfield, New Jersey, to Meet John O'Donnell, the closest person I knew as an Alfa Romeo expert. I had already met John, a heating oil salesman who made a sideline business of buying European cars advertised in the Sunday edition of the *New York Times*, or sometimes buying from Bart Loyens, a broker in Luxembourg. Those that he bought from Loyens were usually non-runners that he bought cheaply and brought them into the United States through the nearby Port of New York. John wasn't a collector. He usually dismantled the cars and sold parts to the relatively few people who were interested in such cars in those days. And John seemed to know them all. John was a friendly, easy-going Irishman who, like me, loved reading about these cars.

Jackie and I took John and his wife to dinner, and that was fun. We became instant friends. I had talked on the phone to John about this Alfa that I had found, and at dinner he assured me that it was worth more as parts than the $2,500 asking price. So armed with high hopes and John's opinion, we left the next day for Corning, where the vacation part began. I was president of the National Electric Sign Association that year, and we had an invitation to come to Corning for a tour of the glass works. We were houseguests of Bob Lambert and his wife Jean, who lived in nearby Painted Post. Bob was a vice president of Corning Glass, which made all the neon glass tubing in North America. We had a wonderful time and became lifelong friends with the Lamberts as a result of that trip. We were given the red-carpet treatment of the glass works, including the plant where the glass tubing was drawn, which was off-limits to most visitors. We also visited the Steuben Art Glass works where some of the world's finest art glass objects are made. The next day, a Sunday, following a fine lunch at the famous Tavern on the Green, we left for the tiny village of Wayland, to finally see a real 8C Alfa Romeo.

When we arrived in the afternoon I was surprised to see a tiny frame house with no garage. I knocked on the door and was greeted by the owner of the Alfa, a truck driver by trade. I could not help wondering why a truck driver, who obviously lived in very modest circumstances, would have one of the great, supercharged Alfa Romeo automobiles. He took me around the house to where the Alfa was parked—under a tree! My heart sank because what I saw was a far, far different image than the one I had conjured up mentally from all my reading. And that was just the beginning. His ad had said the car could be driven anywhere. As it turned out it couldn't be driven anywhere at all—not even from where it was parked under the tree in the back yard, where it had been parked for years. It was half-full of leaves and moss was growing on the floor! In spite of a new battery the owner couldn't even start it. Also, the hand-made aluminum body was built over an ash wood frame that had mostly disintegrated. The whole upper half of the body could be moved around like a bowl of jelly. And it was ugly! This surprised me for I had never seen a picture of an *ugly* Alfa.

Naturally I had called the man before we ever left Colorado to tell him we were coming to look at the car. I could not believe that anyone wanting to sell a car would not have at least cleaned the leaves and moss out of the car, and would have made sure it would at least run. It was now dusk and we went into the house. While Jackie and his wife talked, he told me how he came by the car. It had been driven in the first post-war American Grand Prix at Watkins Glen, he said, in 1948, probably as a token, since it was not a racecar. It was left there at Smalley's Garage to sell. It sat outside for years until the truck driver bought it for next to nothing. Sadly, I told him I was not interested in the car. He asked if I would care to make an offer. I said no, since there was no way to know the condition of the engine and drivetrain if the car would not run. It was now almost dark, and we drove away.

Jackie could tell how disappointed I was. After about an hour of silence, I stopped the car and told Jackie that if I left the car there, it would slowly molder into the ground. Remembering what John O'Donnell said about the value for parts, I stopped at a phone booth and called him back. I offered $1,000 for the car on the condition he could find a tow truck driver who would take it to Corning that night. Even though it was a Sunday evening, he called me back to say yes, and yes. When we got back to his house, the tow truck was just winching the car up onto the road. Following the truck, we finally got back to Corning after midnight, and parked the car in the service driveway of a sports-car dealer I had spotted there. I left a note on the windshield asking them to see if they could start the car.

Next day, Bob Lambert and I went to the service manager, who had done nothing but move it out of his way. We soon found that no fuel was reaching the carburetor. After we rigged up a can of gas with a hose so gas would flow by gravity to the carburetor, it started instantly with a roar, because beyond the original headers the exhaust pipes and muffler had rusted away. Bob Lambert thought I was out of my mind until he heard that mighty engine come to life. Then he said he thought I was just deranged a bit. It had good oil pressure, so I was at least assured the engine was essentially intact and restorable. What to do now? Bob offered to help in any way he could, using the mighty Corning Glass works shops as necessary.

Nowadays, this would be no problem at all. There are at least a dozen big automobile transport companies, with fleets of enclosed trucks that make a business of transporting collectable automobiles. But there were none then. I decided to tow the car home, and Bob had his shop weld up and fit a tow-bar to the front axle. Then I did one of the most stupid things I have ever done; I bought a little used Triumph TR-4 sports car to pull it with! I could have bought an old Cadillac or some similar big car for the same money, but I reasoned I could sell the TR-4 for what I paid for it when I got it home. I towed the Alfa while Jackie followed me back to Newark, to return our rental car, and we took off, looking like the Joad family from *The Grapes of Wrath*. The only thing we lacked was a mattress on top! The TR-4 was anything but comfy for a long trip, even without towing another car. It was gutsy enough to pull the Alfa, even though the Alfa was bigger and heavier than the Triumph, but every time we had to stop, we could feel the Alfa pushing the roadster and I could see Jackie's white knuckles on the TR-4's grab-bar. Up to now, Jackie had been a real sport about this fiasco, but in Zanesville, Ohio, she said, "OK, I've had it! It's either the Alfa or me! I'm taking a bus, a train, or a plane, but I'm not going another foot in this Rube Goldberg contraption!" When I paused to ponder my options, she *really* got mad! I called around and found the only way I could get the car home from Zanesville was by Mayflower van. I unhooked the car at their dock, signed the papers and we took off in the TR-4 for home. For the next couple of days, every now and then, Jackie would mention something about Bermuda, and I would point out the cardinals and beautiful flowers we were seeing on the Kentucky turnpike. The rest of the trip home was pleasant enough, but we were both mighty tired of that TR-4 by the time we got home. Our butts were never the same! But I did sell it for what I paid for it.

Much later I learned a good deal about this Alfa's history. It was called a Sports Saloon with a custom body built by Boneschi. It was originally sold to Gian Cassola in December 1933. The price was 86,000 lira, equal to $5,775 then or $82,000 now. Mr. Cassola kept the car twelve years until the end of the war when it was sold May 12, 1945. Through his connections Luigi Chinetti got it out of Italy for John Cuccio, an industrial designer, who drove it a for quite a while. He sold it to J. Cameron Peck, who had a substantial automobile collection. The car went through a number of owners including Al Trager, G. Barratt in Canada and Frank Griswold, a well-known racing driver and Alfa specialist who left it with Smalley's Garage to be sold, and finally the truck driver who parked it under his tree.

A neon sign manufacturing plant has most of the equipment and the skilled people that are needed to restore a car. I had about thirty employees at that time. I decided to restore this Alfa "in-house" as much as possible. Ron Kerr, my plant superintendent, was an extraordinarily talented craftsman, and wanted to do most of the work for me in the plant, evenings and weekends, for his regular hourly wage. I agreed and worked alongside of him much of the time.

Most Alfa Romeos left the factory as a running chassis, and the buyer had a custom body made by his choice of carrozzerie (body designer-builders). Because most of the wood in this body was totally rotten I had no reservations about restyling the body by using the hood and the rear body tub and reshaping the original fenders and doors. I made several sketches, then a full size side and plan view for Ron to follow. I put the

BEFORE

Home at last! Now What?

full size drawing on the big pattern-wall in our sign plant so that Ron could measure everything full size.

Ron and I dismantled the car completely, right down to the bare frame. I did much of the dirty work and refinishing, while Ron concentrated on the bodywork and the mechanical restoration.

With an eighteen bearing crankshaft, hemispherical combustion chambers, double overhead camshafts driven by a cascading tower of nine gears in the center of the engine, straight-through intake and exhaust porting and dry-sump lubrication, these Alfa chassis were designed for sports-car and grand prix racing but they were also tractable enough for ordinary street use.

In the engine, transmission, rear axle and brakes, everything possible was made of beautifully formed or cast aluminum to save weight. I now understood why 8C-2.3 Alfas were held in such high esteem all over the world. Henry Ford reputedly said, "When I see an eight-cylinder Alfa Romeo, I take off my hat!" If it could be said that a human could fall in love with a mechanical thing, I fell in love with this wonderful piece of beautiful Italian machinery.

I farmed out the engine machine work for which we were not equipped. I also had new pistons made to the original pattern, but raised the compression ratio from 5:75 to 6:00 to 1. I had the supercharger rebuilt by Bandimier, who were racecar mechanics in Denver at that time, and who

The crankcase, head and eighteen-bearing crankshaft.

later promoted the famous Bandimier drag-racing strip near Denver. This was originally promoted as a way to keep kids from racing their hotrods on the streets of Denver at night. They could bring their hopped up cars to the strip on weekends and race them in competition under safer, supervised conditions.

We dismantled every mechanical component, cleaned it, rebuilt or refinished it as necessary and reassembled it. We replaced every bearing, bushing and seal in the car. Ron rebuilt the suspension system and machined new bronze bushings for the spring shackles. He dismantled the

Starting from the bare, sandblasted and repainted frame.

leaf springs and ground out the wear where the leaf-ends rubbed, so they would flex freely. He had them re-arched, then he gun-blued the springs for appearance and to prevent rusting. I dismantled the wire wheels and had them rebuilt in Denver. We chrome plated the rims and put in new stainless steel spokes. Unlike the present, finding new tires of this size was a problem. I finally found a set of tires in the U.S. that were made in Australia, where a lot of old cars were still in service.

Little by little the chassis was coming together. I found that I really enjoyed learning from Ron how things were done, but it was up to me to find the specifications and drawings from the manufacturers if they were available. John O'Donnell was my source for these for the Alfa. He had a rare copy of the original factory parts manual, and sent me a photocopy of the illustrations. These illustrations were invaluable. Each component, such as the supercharger for instance, had a perspective illustration of the whole unit, and also had an exploded perspective assembly drawing, showing every part in its sequence of assembly, and the part name, in Italian of course. I kept an Italian to English dictionary close by; if Ron needed a name I gave him its English equivalent. These illustrations of every part in the whole chassis, down to the tiniest washer, amazed me. I thought of the countless hours the factory's illustrators had spent doing these wonderfully executed illustrations for a model of which only 188 would ever be produced!

The running chassis. This is how they left the factory to have the body fitted.

The challenges of finding the people and resources that could do the work we could not do or for which we did not have the equipment were also left up to me. Ron polished most of the aluminum parts that were visible in the engine compartments. I repainted all the chassis and body components, as they were ready for assembly. Since we had no guidance, we used our own judgment when decisions had to be made regarding originality and authenticity. I knew that restoring a custom-bodied Alfa Romeo was not like restoring a production model of a classic car like a Cadillac or Packard. For instance, when we saw that the original factory finish on a metal part was prone to rust, we chose to improve the finish to prevent future rusting while still using the original part. All of the steel metric bolts and nuts that were exposed, we had cadmium plated. If the threads are not protected, this makes it hard to fit the nuts over the plated threads, so we would run a die over the plated threads to help the nuts seat easily. As another example of a modification we made, the aluminum fenders could be dented by stones thrown up by the tires, so we laminated a thin layer of fiberglass to the underside of the fenders. This also strengthened them to prevent future metal fatigue, which is a big problem of these old hand-beaten aluminum body parts. And to strengthen some of the new wood joints in concealed areas where they were fitted to the remaining wood that was usable, especially on the door jambs, we laminated fiberglass around the joints to prevent movement and separation. When the car was finished, there was not a single squeak or rattle on the car!

In 1967 I published a little registry booklet of every known 8C-2.3 Alfa owner in the world that I could find. Out of the original 188 cars that had been manufactured, I believe I included just over 80 cars and owners. Most were in England, and even the cars in New Zealand, South Africa and Australia were owned by people of the British Commonwealth. There were 33 in the U.S. and there were even a few in South America where they had been left after racing in Argentina. I had the only 8C 2.3 Alfa in Colorado and I knew of only four in California, the automobile Mecca of the West. Without exaggeration one could safely say they were rare! I was traveling on business a lot in those days, and made it a point to meet other 8C Alfa owners when I could. I met owners in New York, Connecticut, New Jersey, Ohio, Illinois, Michigan and California, and James Ibold of Cincinnati came to see me!

By December 1965 we had a complete, running chassis, which I was able to drive wearing a heavy coat and a motorcycle helmet with a visor. These engines had no belts or chains. Everything was gear-driven for reliability. With no floorboards or body, I could see, feel and hear the singing of every mechanical part of this double overhead cam supercharged racing engine and the bevel-cut gears in the racing transmission! I was absolutely thrilled to hear those lovely mechanical sounds, all as they should be, but when pushed they began to tell anyone who heard—this is an engine built for racing!

This is the way they usually left the factory—for about $9,500 in 1932 ($135,000 in 2005 dollars!) The instrument panel was part of the chassis so all the wiring and controls were complete in this form. The bodies were built to bolt to the frame. As we did the restoration over a nine-month period, I began corresponding with other 8C-2.3 Alfa Romeo owners all over the world. I had the U.S. club member list and I had joined the Alfa Romeo section of the English Sports Car Club as a starting point. They had about 40 or more 8C-2.3 Alfa owner members. With names and addresses as my first contacts by mail, I found that the English owners always answered their mail, even the few who were Lords.

Ron Kerr enjoyed restoring the Alfa so much that he asked if I would consider having him leave his position as shop superintendent of my sign plant to do restoration work for me full time. After serious thought I decided to continue doing this, not as a business for profit, but as a means of investing in unrestored cars that I would buy, restore and sell after owning them at least long enough to qualify for capital gains on any profit I might make. I sought the advice of my CPA to be certain I was doing it right. I got a Colorado dealer license, for tax reasons, and registered the name Exotic Car Store. But I was never a broker or dealer in the usual

The 1933 8C-2300 Alfa Romeo, chassis number 2311235.

sense. I was always a restorer, and with three exceptions, described later, we only restored cars that I owned.

I had just completed a new addition to my sign plant where Exotic Car Store rented a separate 30' × 40' room for the car shop. This was great for me. I could take a few minutes' break from my busy schedule a couple of times a day, go to the car shop and keep closely aware of what was going on, and "see if there were any tracks in the dust." Restoration work is painfully slow. However, I never placed any time or cost constraints on a project. I wanted to do the very best work we could and take my chances on making a profit or a loss when the car was sold. For the next 25 years I employed first Ron Kerr, then, after Ron retired, Loran Swanson in a full time endeavor. I found that a difficult frame-up restoration required about 2000 man-hours, or a year's work. In addition, such things as engine machine work, all the plating, wheeling new aluminum body parts and the leather upholstering were farmed out. While waiting for outside vendors or parts, I found that I needed to have at least two and sometimes three cars at a time in progress to keep my man busy.

The restyled body turned out very well, and was more typical of Alfa body styling. The seats were rebuilt with new springs and trimmed with black leather. Ron reshaped the cowl and made the fold-down windshield castings. I made the new "Monza" style radiator shroud. The car was a thrill to drive. With less than two turns, lock-to-lock, the steering was very quick and precise. The trick was to hold the steering wheel lightly and not saw the steering back and forth. The car was very responsive in every way. It was my first right hand drive car, but I soon became so accustomed to it that I was perfectly at home when switching between left-hand or right-hand drive cars. The accelerator pedal was between the clutch and brake pedals, and all three were close together so that the throttle and brake or clutch pedals could be used in a "heel and toe" fashion by those more skilled than I was. The left hand shifted the four-speed and reverse transmission. It was a non-synchronized "crash" box. After I had driven the car a lot, I could shift up or down very fast and cleanly without using the clutch by catching the engine speed just right. I imagine the professional drivers shifted a lot without the clutch. The big, rod-operated finned aluminum brakes had shrunk-in steel liners, and they would really stop the car. The easy way to tell a six cylinder Alfa

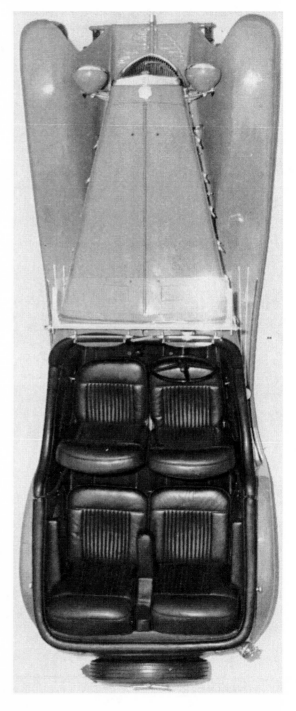

The long chassis with roomy leather seating for four people.

from an eight cylinder Alfa is to look at the brakes through the wire wheels. The 8C brake drums fill the wheels entirely. The 6C's do not.

In standard tune the 143 cubic inch displacement engine produced 140 hp, with a top speed of about 110 mph. The short chassis Mille Miglia cars with a somewhat higher tune would do about 120 mph, and the bored-out 2.6-liter Grand Prix engines produced about 165 hp at 5,000 rpm and simply dominated GP racing. Yet these were all basically the same engines. The MM cars had larger valves and slightly higher blower boost. The Gran Prix cars had higher compression ratios, bigger valves, Weber carburetors and yet more blower boost. But for me, it was a real pleasure just to look at the engine. It was like jewelry, inside and out.

The most sought after 8C Alfas were those with a racing history. Enzo Ferrari managed the factory-sponsored Alfa racing team. Scuderia Ferrari tuned and modified them and hired great drivers like Nuvolari, Compari, Varzi, Borzacchini and many others who dominated Gran Prix racing prior to the war. My car was a long chassis model, with no racing history, but other than restyling the body, it was an absolutely original chassis. In some respects, an Alfa that was just a touring car was better because it was never used very hard. Some, like mine, showed very little wear on the mechanical parts.

The modified Boneschi body turned out well, but all for naught.

In 1968 I sold my car at Sotheby's Auction in Denver for $18,000, which would amount to $129,000 in 2005 inflated dollars. The buyer was not present but was bidding by phone. To my knowledge, that was the highest price ever paid for an Alfa up to that time. Judging by recent multi-million dollar prices paid for these supercharged straight eight Alfas, it would probably bring about $1.5 million today. I had a total of $9,000 invested, so I made 100 percent over my cost, and was taxed at the rate for capital gains, which was 20 percent at that time. I assumed that when the selling price was made public it would raise the value of restored cars, so I was anxious to purchase an unrestored short chassis car as soon as possible. I already had one located and lost no time to fly to Cincinnati to see it.

The Alfa Monza chassis # 2211097 in Cincinnati appeared to be a genuine Monza chassis, but was in very bad shape, needing a total restoration. It had been rebodied at least once and its history was uncertain. The asking price of $7,500 plus what I knew the restoration would cost would make it too expensive, so I turned it down. In view of today's prices that was a very big mistake. But that was all it was worth then! Peter Giddings, who had moved from England to New York, later bought that car and rebuilt it using the same body.

When I learned that Mr. James Lexvold of St. Charles, Illinois, was the buyer of my car at the auction I wrote to him and sent him the history of the car with photographs of its restoration. He was thrilled with the car and enjoyed taking his family on pleasant drives in the countryside around St. Charles. It saddens me to say that the Alfa, along with the rest of his small collection of quality cars, was destroyed in a fire. The cars were kept on the upper floor of a two story oak-timbered barn on his country estate. I went to see the remains in hopes that some of the parts could be salvaged. It was totally destroyed. So many of these Alfas' components are made of aluminum that it was nothing more than a molten slag of aluminum over an oak beam, with a twisted crankshaft hanging in the middle, and a twisted steel chassis frame that could never be rebuilt. *Requiem.*

Today my restored long-chassis Alfa would have had a market value of $1,500,000 and the genuine Monza that I turned down for $7,500, after a restoration and with a proper replica body, would be worth from $4,000,000 to $5,000,000 according to the latest Sports Car Market Price Guide.

2

The Jaguars
(and a Few Others)

While we were rebuilding the 8C-2.3 Alfa, I had been reading about all the contemporary high-performance cars, and especially about the fabulous XKE Jaguars that were then in the showrooms of the British sports car dealers in Denver and Boulder. I thought the E-Type Jaguars were the most beautiful production cars in the world and I really wanted to buy one, but I couldn't afford to spend $4,500 for a sports car just for my personal use. That would require a second car for my family transportation. That didn't keep me from lusting. I also read about the next best thing to an XKE, which was the Jaguar Mark II sedan that had the same beautiful inline six-cylinder engine, with only slightly less power. While on a business conference in Minneapolis, I bought a nice used 1962 Mark II saloon with the 3.8 liter engine. It had all leather seats and door panels, with real wood garnish rails, pull down wood picnic vanities for the rear passengers in the front seat backs, and a very attractive instrument panel full of gauges. The Mark II to own is one with knock-off wire wheels and with a manual transmission and the electric overdrive. They are much better than those with the Borg Warner automatic that were pretty bad in those days. Mine had all that good stuff. What I liked best was its compact body style that had absolutely no surplus sheet metal overhang in either the front or back, yet had an adequate trunk for all but a serious vacation.

The only thing I did to this car was to repaint it. I drove it for quite a while as my everyday transportation. The handling and performance, compared to contemporary American cars, were in a completely different

The 1962 Mark II 3.8 liter Jaguar Sport Saloon. I wish I had it now!

class. I vowed that I would never own another American family car until Detroit began building better cars. A little knowledge is a dangerous thing; I had become a car snob. This is about the same time that Lee Iacocca, then with Ford Motor Company, began to complain about the "unfair competition" coming from Japan, when foreign cars had taken about 10 percent of the American market. I wrote him a letter explaining why I chose to buy foreign cars based on their better handling, brakes and suspension systems. My son-in-law, Tom Haynie, bet that I would not get a reply. I told him that people do not become corporate presidents by not answering their mail, and sure enough I got an answer. Mr. Iacocca said that the real reason Japan was taking a market share was price. He chose not to address the handling, suspension, braking or performance issues. I'm very happy to say that many of today's American cars compete very favorably in terms of handling, but Detroit waited much too long to answer these issues.

We had four kids that I taught to drive by taking them out on the country roads where hitting anything was less likely. I taught them five things in the following order: how to check the oil and water and why they should, how to shift a manual transmission, how to drive defensively and to keep *lots* of distance between them and anything else, and how to change a flat. In spite of many lectures all of them had minor accidents. I must have done a pretty good job though, because they all became good drivers and none of them has ever had a serious accident. Before I became a total car snob and quit buying American cars entirely, I expressed my rebellion by buying oddball stuff for the kids. I taught Robin, the oldest, to drive in my convertible Corvair Monza with a Paxton supercharger that I installed. If any readers have a Corvair and are considering adding a supercharger, I suggest you forget that! Robin was a good driver, but the driver of a huge hay truck that was parked on the side of the road couldn't see the Corvair approaching and suddenly turned in front of her. The rear of the truck bed caught the Corvair and dragged it into the ditch. But no one was hurt and the truck driver was cited. I was tired of the Corvair anyway and used the insurance money to buy something else. Barbara and Jennifer, number two and three daughters, learned to drive in a party Jeep, one of those cute little two-wheel-drive things they use for tourists in Florida and Hawaii. It was painted pink, with a pink and white surrey top that made it look like an ice cream vendor. They were both learning French, so on each side I lettered in gold leaf "La Grenouille Rose" which is French for *The Pink Frog*. I bought it because it was cheap, but it was also dangerous because of the short wheelbase and poor brakes, so I sold it before winter. Then I gave the girls a used Mercedes diesel, on which I installed a block heater so it would start in the winter. That got them to school safely, but after sitting out in the cold all day, it sometimes wouldn't start after school.

Jennifer was driving an Austin America until she made a left turn and was creamed by a driver coming from behind a semi. Neither one could see the other. Again, no one was hurt but the Austin was totaled. The 1961 Peugeot 404 that followed was the best car I ever gave the girls to drive to school. It was reliable; it had a manual transmission, it always started, it had good brakes and provided everything a school kid needed except glamour. I sold it to my nephew, Dick Brooks, who had just married Kathy Schuster, a beautiful local girl. Dick was in the Army, undergoing basic training at Fort Polk, Louisiana. Jackie and I were going to a sign association meeting at the Lake of the Ozarks. We drove Kathy that far in the Peugeot but she still had a hundred miles to go. Kathy had never driven a stick shift, so I gave her a ten-minute lesson, and the last we saw of her she was jerking and jumping the Peugeot down the street, trying to master the clutch, gearshift lever and the brakes, but she made it.

By this time I was so prejudiced against American cars I bought Jackie a very nice used Austin Healy Mark III for her everyday car. She let Barbara drive it to school a few times, and Barbara later said that it was a real boy getter but never actually got her a date. It was so low to the ground that Jackie couldn't drive it in more than four inches of snow. So on a trip to Chicago, I traded an Alfa dealer some Water Pic stock for a new Alfa Romeo Sprint Speciale for Jackie, and drove it home from Chicago to break it in. Then, while I was in Philadelphia, I bought a very nice used Alfa Romeo Giulietta Spider Veloce for myself. I drove it across country in mid-winter and almost froze to death! I guess it doesn't get cold enough in Italy to need a heater that actually gets warm. I blocked off the frigid air to the radiator with cardboard, but it helped very little. I had just finished the 8C-2.3 Alfa, so for a short time, we had three Alfa Romeos.

Then poor Brian, our one and only boy-child, reached the driving age of sixteen at this very time when we had nothing but foreign cars. The first day he got his license, without my permission he took my little Alfa Romeo Spyder Veloce to Cheyenne without checking the oil. I'm sure he was driving too fast and, you guessed it—he burned out a rod. His two older sisters were now married so I could afford to get him a well-used Volvo 1800S. He was driving that when suddenly the engine caught fire. The neoprene gas line came loose at the carburetor and gasoline on the

Surely this six-cylinder Buick is beyond saving!

hot exhaust caught fire. When he turned the ignition off the gas stopped coming and fortunately the fire went out. Brian was so upset he swore he would never drive again. Probably most of these misfortunes happened to my kids because their father was out of his mind when it came to cars!

At that time, antique cars were very popular, defined at that time by the Antique Automobile Club of America as any car built before 1930. Ron needed something to fill in when he was waiting for some part or outside service, and he found a derelict six-cylinder 1917 Buick roadster. I bought it for a few hundred dollars. It was in such sorry shape that I didn't think Ron could do much for it. The rear of the body had been cut off to convert the car into a small flatbed truck. The cut-off part came with the car, however. I didn't pay a lot of attention to it until Ron had the body back in one piece, made new wood for the steering wheel, and rebuilt the engine. I then took enough interest to paint the car and select the leather for a new interior. It was a surprising transformation when Ron finished it. It also surprised by how well it ran for a World War I vintage car. But it was not my cup of tea. I don't even remember to whom I sold it.

I had a restaurateur customer in Fort Collins who had a low mileage 1964 E-Type coupe. He needed a sedan, so I traded my Mark II on his gorgeous XKE. With its great handling and performance it was the best car I had ever owned up to that time. At six feet and 175 pounds then, I

The 1917 Buick—not too bad after all!

The 1964 1st Series E-Type Jaguar Coupe.

found the legroom tight, but I would have put up with any amount of dis-comfort to have that car. The deck space behind the seats was roomy enough for luggage but the Jaguar would not have been good for really long, cross-country driving for a large person. However, I didn't use it that way. We had purchased another neon sign plant in Cheyenne, Wyoming, 50 miles from Fort Collins, and I made a trip up there at least twice a week. I would frequently drive from Cheyenne over I-80 to Laramie then back to Fort Collins down highway 287. This was a trip of about 150 miles over a lot of scenic terrain and was a real pleasure in the XKE.

However, it didn't take long to get acquainted with Lucas, the "Prince of Darkness." It seemed that something was always going wrong with the cheap electrical components Lucas provided for Jaguars. It wasn't as if Lucas couldn't build good electrical components. They also were used in Rolls-Royce, but obviously those parts were of better quality. They say a Rolls-Royce never breaks down, but sometimes they do fail to proceed. The windshield washer/wiper motor, the tachometer sending unit mounted on the rear of the cam-box, the generator and starter were all subject to frequent problems. Lucas built the fuel pumps, too, and most of the British cars had two of them in hopes that at least one would work long enough to get you home. Most owners of British cars kept a 10-inch spanner (British Whitworth, of course) under the driver's seat. They could open the door, lean out, reach under the car and use the wrench to bang on the fuel pump conveniently mounted there to the frame. This would un-stick the points and you could go again.

And if it wasn't Lucas, it was Smiths, the maker of those seductive, white on black-faced instruments that would mysteriously just stop

working. The saucer-size speedometer was as much as 20 percent opti-
mistic, if it worked at all. I used to say that if the British automobile industry had driven Smiths and Lucas into the sea they would still rule the
world. At least it was very convenient to undo the two black plastic knurled
nuts to allow the beautiful instruments to hinge down, thereby exposing
the lovely wiring harness and fuse panel. I always kept a glove box full of
fuses, especially the 50 amp one, which controlled just about everything.

But regardless of the Lucas and Smiths problems, the XKE was a
beautiful and wonderful car to drive. When first introduced in 1961 they
created a sensation at all the auto shows. It was a very advanced chassis
design, developed from Jaguar's racing experience with the C- and D-Types,
with the rear de Dion swing-axle differential and big inboard disc brakes
all mounted on a removable subframe. Four big tubular shocks and coil
springs made for an impressive rear suspension that resulted in an outstanding ride with good handling for its time. Front suspension was also independent with a-arms, coil springs and tubular shocks. The disc brakes,
very precise rack and pinion steering, and that beautiful, wonderful 4.2 liter
double overhead cam engine, with three big SU carburetors producing 265
hp were simply awesome for a car at such a relatively low price. The engine
and front suspension were mounted on a lightweight tubular frame that
bolted to plates built into the monocoque body. The mechanical parts of
the car were strong and reliable, having been developed from the race-
proven C- and D-Types that won Le Mans several consecutive times. For
such sophisticated design, it was relatively easy to work on. The whole front
end could be removed if necessary, but was also very accessible with the
long, front-hinged hood lifted. Top speed depended on the axle ratio, but
with tall gearing it would do 150 mph. U.S. models would easily do about
135 mph. And it sold for less than half the price for a Ferrari, Maserati or
Aston Martin.

Under the hood of the XKE Roadster.

The early cars, from 1961 through 1963, had a rather clunky gearbox that was synchronized only on the two top gears, but a new, all-synchro transmission was available for the 1964 models. All three of my XKEs had the later gearbox, which I found to be very nice. As time passed, rust became a problem for cars that were exposed to snow, ice and road salt. The floor pans and fender wells are the most susceptible areas. New reproduction sheet metal parts are now available for restoration projects. I believe the Series One cars, those built through 1967, are the ones to have.

I think the overall aesthetics of the XKE are what kept me coming back to them. If the car had nothing more to offer than the gorgeous body styling, it would have been a great car. But the design and finish of the entire drivetrain of the car was given great care and thought for aesthetic consideration. The polished aluminum cam covers with chrome plated acorn nuts, and the polished carburetor dashpots, plus the porcelain enameled six-branch exhaust headers were the jewelry.

But I eventually tired of frequently having to fix some Lucas or Smiths gadget and I sold the very nice E-Type coupe to an upwardly mobile young couple from Denver who promised they would love and care for the car forever. While I was glad to get back to a Mercedes sedan, I never really got over the looks and the feel of driving the XKE. So of course I eventually had to have two more, both 1967 models, the last production year before Federal regulation began to ruin the XKE, aesthetically and in terms of performance. My second was a fine, restored car that I took in trade on a 250GT Ferrari with a Boano coupe body, in 1979. A restored '67 XKE

The beautiful 1967 XKE Roadster. Even when the Lucas stuff didn't work it was pretty.

roadster that had sold new for about $4,500 was worth $12,000 by 1979. I kept and drove this car for two years when I sold it to a doctor.

Some people are able to put up with the XKE's foibles, but I suppose I'm too much of a perfectionist. Eventually, every XKE Jaguar I had would begin to harass me with its small niggling problems, for which the cost of parts to fix them wasn't so small, and I would sell it in a fit of pique. But like a beautiful girl, they remained always in my mind. I kept forgetting their faults and remembering their beauty.

Shortly after the Mark X Sedan was introduced, I bought an absolutely pristine example from a man who no doubt was also tired of Lucas and Smiths. It had been driven only 10,000 miles. We took a family vacation to the mouth of the Columbia River in Chinook, Washington, where Jackie's parents lived. I had recently taught Barbara, our number two daughter, to drive. I let her take over for a couple of hours through the Grand Teton country in Wyoming. I wanted her to experience the difference between the handling of a Jaguar and the Jeep she drove to school. This was a beautiful car when it was new, but knowing that Jaguars of that era deteriorated rapidly I drove it for about 10,000 miles and sold it. They

Dave Garroway's SS 100 Jaguar. It looked fast just sitting still.

were fine mechanically, but they were built down to a price for the export market. Surely, the cost of using higher quality electrical components and instruments could not have added much to the cost of these otherwise wonderful cars. William Lyons was a marketing genius who had impeccable aesthetic taste. He relied on the beautiful lines of his cars and outstanding value for price to sell all he could build. In fact, at a time when England needed income, he sold so many cars that the Queen knighted him, after which he was Sir William!

I had had my fill of Jaguars for the rest of my life. Until, that is, about thirty years later when, on a beautiful day, I happened to see a gleaming black Series 1 XKE roadster in Estes Park, and I realized again how strikingly beautiful they are. And how small! I had never cared for black cars, but that car was so striking I thought it might be nice to have another XKE, this time in black. A good black one proved to be hard to find by that time, but I finally found a black one in New England that had just been rebuilt mechanically. I bought it and completed the restoration. I was struck again by how strong and smoothly they drove. They were remarkable cars to have been introduced in 1961. By this time, a good one was worth about $50,000. I kept it for several years but my greater girth and arthritic joints made getting in and out of the car slow and painful. Most certainly there were no Le Mans starts for me. For the uninitiated, in some of the Le Mans races, the cars were lined up in their starting positions on the circuit and the drivers were all standing some distance across the track from their cars. At the drop of the flag, they had to run across the track, jump in their cars, start them, and begin racing. Occasionally a car would fail to start, and the driver would sit there, furiously taking his frustration out on the poor car and his pit crew!

I never considered any of these Jaguars to be investments, but there is one other Jaguar that has stood the test of time as a collectible, the SS 100. More than any other, it exemplified what a vintage English sports car should look like. Only 308 were built, of which only 118 were the 3.5-liter models. It was also the first of William Lyons' cars to bear the Jaguar name and hood ornament. I was destined to have one of those too. Dave Garroway, who was the first host of the *Today Show* back in the days of 10-inch screen black and white television, was a real car enthusiast. He had this 1939 SS-100 3.5 liter Jaguar, with the huge P-100 headlights. He showed it on TV occasionally and drove it in races around New England, including the first Watkins Glen Grand Prix. One day, I saw an ad in *Road & Track* for Dave Garroway's SS-100.

I called him in Los Angeles to talk to him about it. Satisfied with his description of its condition, I flew out to see it. He was living in a modest house, and had a housekeeper who helped him with his cooking. He had been out of television for a very long time, and he told me he was going blind. He had always worn thick glasses, but now he could hardly see to sign the title. I bought the car for his asking price of $18,000. I could see that it was a sad parting with an old friend for him. I drove it home to Colorado.

Dave said that he had blown the original 3.5-liter push-rod engine, and had installed an XK-140 engine that was much more powerful than the original. The car had no top and I left Hollywood in the afternoon to miss most of the quitting-time traffic. I got a lot of "thumbs-up" from the car culture people as I wound my way from Hollywood, through Los Angeles, and through the Santa Ana River canyon to Corona, Riverside San Bernardino and over Cajon Pass to the high desert. I drove all night to Green River, Wyoming, and nearly froze to death in spite of a heavy coat and wool stocking cap. I was cramped in the car because, like most English sports cars, it did not have enough legroom. The car was pretty crude, with not much more suspension than cart-springs. But it was plenty fast with the 140 hp XK engine. And it was pretty.

Dave Garroway had upholstered the seats in genuine alligator hide that was illegal even to possess by the time I bought it. I figured I could always claim it was imitation alligator hide. I bought a 3.5-liter engine so the car could be put back to its original configuration, but since this was Dave Garroway's car, that he had owned ever since it was new, I didn't feel it was right for me to mess with it. When I eventually sold the car to a young man in Denver a couple years later for $28,000, the spare engine

The cockpit was cramped and the frame prevented any further seat adjustment.

went with it. He kept the car for years, and the last I heard, he had never changed the engine either. I guess it was still Garroway's car.

This car story has a sad ending. About a year after I bought the car from Dave Garroway, I read that he had committed suicide in his home, with a shotgun, as I recall. I wondered if he just couldn't face going blind. He was once a very famous personality, and I found him to be a nice man, but he seemed despondent and down on his luck when I met him.

The 2006 Sports Car Market Price Guide *values the SS 100 Jaguar at $230,000. An excellent XKE Roadster is worth "only" about $125,000 and an equally good XKE Coupe about $60,000. The Mark II is now worth about $40,000.*

3

The De Mola Bodied Alfa

Needing more work for Ron, I saw an ad for a very strange but intriguing car offered for sale for very little money by Paul Hatmon, postmaster of Independence, Missouri. It had a custom one-off body built by De Mola in Brussels, fitted to a 6C-1750 supercharged Alfa chassis. An American service man found it in Tunisia, brought it home after the war and "improved" it by fitting a flathead Ford engine and running gear. I went to see it and bought it for $2,100 with the intention of finding a 6C-1750 chassis and turning it back into an Alfa again. Regardless, I knew the body alone was worth more than the asking price.

From old letters Mr. Hatmon gave me with the car I located Umberto De Mola, who, amazingly, was still living in Brussels. I sent him photos of the car as it was when I bought it, and he sent me the original black and white negatives of his body construction in 1939 and the finished car as it was in 1940. He said the body was built of 1mm steel over a light tubular frame. The Cord that had them in 1936 no doubt inspired the flip-up headlights. The full front fender skirts were not very practical as they would limit the turning of the front wheels, but they gave the car a wild shape. It also had pushbutton door locks instead of exposed handles. The bumpers were hand-made of heavy gauge steel. The whole body was an amazing work of a master craftsman. It took several awards at car salons in Europe when it was first shown.

This type of lightweight tubular frame was a great advance over the use of ash wood frames that had been used by most European coachbuilders, especially in England and France. The wood joints would shrink in time and loosen which caused the body to develop squeaks. Inevitably

30

The De Mola body as I bought it.

the wood developed rot, usually long before the useful life of the car's mechanical and metal body parts had expired. This is one reason so many bodies that were originally built over ash frames were rebodied, sometimes more than once. Another reason was metal fatigue, especially in those cars with aluminum bodies for which the panels were formed by beating the metal over sandbags or wooden bucks.

I considered shipping the body to Brussels and having Mr. De Mola reconstruct the body, but the costs were prohibitive. To rebuild the car I bought a complete 6C-1750 Supercharged Gran Turismo Alfa chassis, with no body, from John O'Donnell. When we restored the Gran Turismo chassis to a very high standard, it turned out so well that we decided to build a new replica Zagato style aluminum body for it. I then purchased a less valuable 1948 6C-2500 SS Alfa Farina bodied Cabriolet on which to mount the De Mola body. It was in very good condition, but we had no use for the body when we removed it, so I sold it for salvage. I groan as I write this in 2005, because the unblown Alfa Cabriolet would be worth about $300,000 today, but it was only worth $1000 then.

The fantastic space-frame and body on the streets of Belgium.

The refinished body on a restored 6C-2500 SS Alfa Romeo chassis.

The postwar 2500 SS Alfa was originally a fine car, with a double overhead cam six cylinder engine with three side-draft carburetors. It had torsion bar suspension with expensive hydraulic shock absorbers. In naturally aspirated form, it produced about 105 hp and was good for about 95 mph with its heavy bodywork. At that time they were undervalued as collectibles because the fabulous prewar supercharged eight cylinder Alfas overshadowed them. We rebuilt the engine, stripped and refinished the entire chassis of that car and modified the frame enough to fit the De Mola

At Beaulieu, Umberto De Mola meets up with the body he built in 1940!

The car looks pretty in blue, but with whitewall tires?

body. Ron had to make a missing front bumper and a rear bumper to match. He made these from large diameter EMT (electrical conduit) by bending it first, then splitting the ends, welding and grinding, filing and finally chrome plating them. When Ron finished it, the entire chassis and running gear was at least all Alfa Romeo. My son-in-law, Tom Haynie, nicknamed it the "Batmobile" and was convinced that I would never get my cost out of this one. When an ad with a photo in *Old Cars* drew only one prospect, I began to think Tom was right. I had $8,000 invested and ultimately sold it to a man in Atlanta for $11,000. I later learned that the buyer, who told me he wanted the car for himself, was a dealer. He promptly put it in an auction and sold it for $32,500! I should have advertised it more and waited for better offers.

We didn't make the wheel skirts or try to reconstruct the missing mechanism for the flip-up headlights; nor did we chrome plate the wheels, but rather painted them silver, which was the original finish on these wire wheels used on sports and racing cars. It was believed that chrome plating made the spokes brittle and therefore unsafe for the stresses placed on the spokes in racing.

I lost track of the car until 1982 when I was very pleasantly surprised to receive a letter from Michael Ware, curator of the National Motor Museum at Beaulieu, in England, which now had the car on loan from the Sutton Place Heritage Trust. After extensive correspondence with me to get the straight story, Michael Ware wrote a very nice article telling the correct history, complete with photos, that was published in England's *Classic and Sports Car* magazine. However, the best possible ending to this story was when Umberto De Mola, at age 72, by invitation from the museum, came to England in 1982 to see the body that he had built so many years ago.

But wait, there's even more! In the 1990s another owner showed the car at Pebble Beach. It was repainted and retrimmed in blue, with white-wall tires (!). Perhaps because the history was not passed on from the Sutton Place Heritage Trust to this owner, he claimed that the body was built by a totally different builder and was on its original chassis. I contacted him, gave him the correct history, and as proof, loaned him De Mola's black and white negatives of the car, as it was when it was first built in Brussels. Then, in October of 1995, I received a letter from Jurgen Bremer of Stuttgart, returning the negatives to me. He had purchased the car from Dieter Dambacher. He also sent a photo of the car being driven in the Italian Mille Miglia (1000 mile) vintage race-car event, now held in Italy every year, attracting qualified automobiles from all over the world. Several of the cars that I restored have been accepted to drive in the Mille Miglia, and some have completed it several times.

I get a lot of satisfaction nowadays, well into my eighties, to know that I saw something very special in so many of these cars long before they became valuable. And I got a lot of pleasure in restoring them as best we could, sometimes at a loss. So the story of the "Batmobile," as my son-in-law and I still refer to the car, goes on. By now, the "Batmobile" has probably outlived Mr. De Mola. (He would be 95 now.) And it will outlive me—and who knows how many more owners. And who knows how much more of its history will be changed. Perhaps the story of just this one car illustrates why it has been such a fascinating hobby and pastime for me. And oh yes, I did make a $3,000 profit on it when I sold it!

The only way a value can be established for a one-off bodied car like this is to put it into a big auction. However, the body is mounted on a genuine Alfa 2500SS chassis, the whole car is restored to a high level and it has been shown at Pebble Beach and completed a Mille Miglia. My guess is that it would bring about $300,000 or more.

4

The 6C-1750 Gran Turismo Con Compressore

Concurrent to finishing the De Mola Alfa, I shipped the 6C-1750 Gran Turismo chassis that we had restored to Jack Henser of Proto Products in Warren, Michigan. He needed the chassis to build and fit a new replica Zagato style aluminum body. I had met Jack Henser through Keith Hellon so I was familiar with his work. He did a beautiful job on the replica

A new body for the 6C-1750 Gran Turismo Con Compressore, chassis no. 101014856.

body, but he had stored it outdoors under a heavy tarp. When we picked it up with our truck we discovered that under the tarp the humid, caustic air in Detroit's industrial area had ruined the paint on the chassis. I raised hell about it with Henser but the damage was done. There was nothing to do but to take it home and remove the body, dismantle it and refinish all the running gear from the frame in order to do it properly.

The 6C-1750 Gran Turismo is a larger, heavier chassis with several features identical to the eight-cylinder cars, including the frame, the bigger transmission, the larger diameter brake drums and split-rim 18" wheels. This chassis, No. 101014856, was intended for fitting much heavier, enclosed bodywork. The small bit of information that was handed down to me with the chassis was that it had originally carried a Castagna Coupe body, and that Mr. D. Paige and Dr. D. P. Rucker previously owned it.

The finished car turned out very well, although the lightweight Zagato replica body was not as pretty as the standard 6C-1750 Zagato spiders. The 18" wheels, higher cowl and taller, vertical radiator dictated the height of the body. This resulted in a taller, non-sloping hood line, which, to my eye, made it out of proportion compared to the lower, sloped radiator Zagato bodies. Still, it was a very handsome and rare car because so few of the supercharged Gran Turismo chassis were built, each probably to special order.

After we advertised the car Arlen Goodwine, the artist that was working for our sign company, sold it in 1973 while I was on vacation. The buyer

Compare the proportions of this car to the original Zagato body on page 141.

purchased it over the phone and had it shipped to California. When it arrived, the buyer complained that it had no carpets on the floor. I sent him a copy of the factory photo of a Zagato roadster to show that they originally just had exposed, v-chamfered aluminum floorboards proving the roadsters originally came without carpeting. In any event, I was later told that the owner made carpets for it and showed the car at Pebble Beach, where it won "Most Elegant Car!" If that is true, I can only say that the judges at Pebble Beach must not have been nearly as picky in 1973 as they are in 2005.

I believe I remember that in 1998, in another very complicated car deal with Don Williams, of the Blackhawk Collection, he told me he was the young guy who bought this Alfa from me, and showed it at Pebble Beach. I had heard nothing more about this car until John de Boer, of Walnut Creek, California, who is valiantly trying to track down all the 6C Alfas, sent me his files. Apparently Don Williams sold the car to a Mr. Hayashi and it went to Japan. Hayashi was buying a lot of cars from the United States when the balance of trade was so much in favor of Japan. The car then apparently came back to the States, for Fantasy Junction advertised it in 1995.

This unusual Alfa GT Con Compressore would have a current market value of about $250,000.

5

The 250MM Ferraris

By the mid–1960s I had read Hans Tanner's book *The Ferrari*, the first I had seen on the marque, which led me to understand the natural progression from Alfa Romeo to the early Ferrari racing machines. Tanner and others stated that when Enzo Ferrari built his first competition cars after the war, he more or less continued development where he had left off for the Alfa Romeo. That was logical. I had also been reading a lot about contemporary Ferraris in *Road & Track* and thought I would like to have one someday. My desire for the supercharged Alfas had not abated one whit, but they were very hard to find, and were becoming more valuable all the time.

Keith Hellon was a great 8C Alfa owner-enthusiast near Chicago. His enthusiasm rubbed off on me every time I was with him. While visiting Keith in 1967 I went with him one evening to Bill Knaus' dealership in Lake Forest, where Keith was teaching a seminar on rebuilding contemporary Alfa engines. While there, I was looking around Knaus' garage and spotted an old Ferrari roadster covered with dust. I asked Bill about it and was told that it was a 1953 Ferrari 250MM Barchetta, #0336MM, that had been raced at Sebring. This car was in very sad condition, but it was all in one piece. The car had never been titled for street use, having only been used for racing. The odometer showed only 6500 kilometers, a little over 4,000 miles, but it was in terrible shape for a car with so little use. It still had its Manufacturer's Statement of Origin, made out to Harry Schell and dated November 1953. It was listed as a reconditioned CORSA, or racing car. There was a bill of sale signed off by Harry Schell as owner. Schell was a well-known driver, having been credited as being the first American to compete in European Grand Prix racing. Bill Knaus also told me Schell and Marquis de Portago drove the car in the 12 Hours of Sebring. Years later I learned that the car was first sold in May 1953 to the Marquis de Portago and that he and Schell drove the car to second place in the 1000 km race at Buenos Aires.

After some haggling I bought it from Knaus for about $4,000 as I recall. It had no windshield, but there was one small, short chrome plated post for a fold-down windshield of some sort. The car was in bad shape, and while it was not running, we at least had the advantage of getting this car in one piece. Knaus arranged shipping by auto carrier and the car arrived shortly after I returned to Colorado.

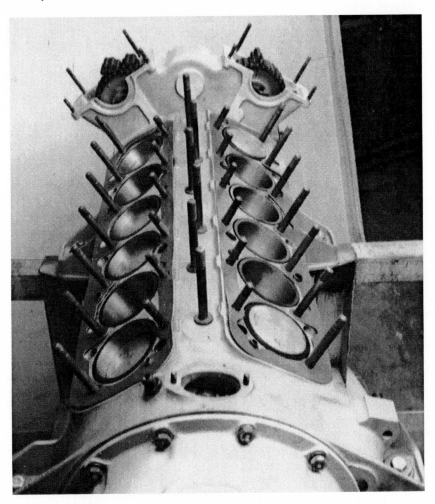

The rebuilt twelve-cylinder block of 1953 250MM #0336.

Without an English language shop manual, this Ferrari engine was a totally new challenge for Ron and me. Letters to the factory for parts or technical data were simply ignored. Tanner's book included illustrations of the Italian parts manual for the same three-liter Colombo-designed twelve-cylinder GT engine, and as we carefully took the engine apart we could see that there were only minor differences between our engine and the illustrations. The book was illustrating the engines that were used in the early street Ferraris several years later than our 1953 engine. I did receive good information from Weber regarding the three four-choke carburetors, with advice on what jet numbers to use for running at our high altitude. The standard specifications were for sea level, and they recommended changing jets for every 2000 feet in altitude. With virtually nothing for guidance, we used our best judgment as to how the engine and drivetrain were originally built.

Through some of my contacts in England I managed to find the proper oversized Vandervell inserts for the main and rod bearings so we could grind the crankshaft to the first standard undersize. Thin-wall insert bearings were one of the most important engine developments that came along just prior to World War II. Prior to insert bearings, the poured babbitt metal for rod and main bearings did not dissipate heat as well, and because it had to be much thicker, it was softer and tended to break up and even-

The restored chassis frame with the aluminum body in progress.

tually fail. High revolutions were only made possible with the advent of these thin steel shells with a very thin surface of bearing metal alloyed with tin. Borgo made the beautiful, lightweight, domed pistons with slipper skirts, so called because they were cut away opposite the wristpins to make them lighter, and they were reinforced inside. They had probably been replaced after racing, as the fit was still close. We had the piston skirts knurled and found new piston rings to fit the pistons. We merely honed the steel liners to break the glaze so the rings would seat properly. I had the original valve stems hard-chromed and ground back to the original size by a specialty grinding company. I was able to scrounge new timing chains, an engine gasket set and new distributor parts from Luigi Chinetti's and Bill Harrah's Ferrari dealerships.

I sandblasted all the metal parts and as Ron rebuilt various chassis components, I would repaint them. It was exciting to see the chassis coming together, looking as new. By brazing new fittings to the original metric threaded parts Ron was able to make up all new hydraulic lines and brake hoses. We turned the brake drums and relined the shoes to rebuild the brake system. Ron rebuilt the transmission with new bearings and seals. Following our practice of replacing every bearing and seal as we went, we found that Ferrari used a few very unusual bearings in the engine and transmission, and they had to come from a dealer, who could order them from Italy.

I helped Ron reassemble the engine, and did the Weber carburetors myself. These were the first Weber carburetors I had ever dismantled. Because there were three identical carburetors, I dismantled them one at a time to be certain I would be able to assemble them correctly. However, I found them to be very simple to work on because all of the jets would only go in one way, and each was of a different size. I soaked the main carburetor housings in lacquer thinner. The jets and accelerator pumps I soaked in carburetor cleaner, which ruined the neoprene O-rings, and I had a devil of a time finding the right metric replacements. Thereafter, I was more careful what parts I put into the potent carburetor cleaner. Once the parts were cleaned, I blew everything out with high-pressure air, then reassembled the carburetors. I bench-tested them by putting gasoline in the float chamber and worked the accelerator lever while looking into the venturi. This only showed that everything was clean and working. The tuning would have to be done with the engine running. I believe Webers are the best carburetors in the world. They are designed with quick-change jets and venturi chokes so that, by changing these parts, one can literally change the power-curve of the engine. For example, maximum torque may be desired if racing on a short, twisting mountain circuit where maximum

power is needed at relatively low speed, whereas for racing on a road circuit like Le Mans or the Mille Miglia maximum power may be needed at
higher speeds. Weber also published literature to help one to understand
their products and how to tune them. I wanted to personally learn as much
about these Ferrari engines as I could, hands-on.

In 1968 I bought a new book titled *Ferrari: The Sports and Gran Turismo Cars*, by Warren Fitzgerald and Richard Merritt. I read it over and
over, gleaning new information about Ferraris to help us with our restoration. Dick Merritt had written that a Ferrari is first and foremost an engine,
and after rebuilding a few and driving them, I could not agree more. I also
learned that any careful, competent mechanic could work on these early
Ferraris if he would take the time to understand them and learn how to
tune the ignition and carburetion system. Once computer electronics and
fuel injection were introduced in automobiles, without factory assistance

The heads mounted with valves and springs before camshafts are installed.

this was no longer true. Of course, just being able to overhaul an engine and get it running reasonably well is probably far short of what the factory trained racing mechanics could do with one of these engines.

The wiring diagram and electrical components were familiar, as they were very similar to the later Alfa Romeos. I had the instruments rebuilt by a specialist in California. We got one small windshield post casting with the Ferrari, and Ron made a duplicate for the other side. He fabricated a fold-down windshield which I'm sure was not like the original, but it looked good and it worked well. The head gaskets for these early engines were nothing more than a perimeter gasket and a series of loose copper and asbestos rings for the top of the piston liners and a bunch of copper/asbestos O-rings for the water ports. The oil ports were neoprene O-rings. All these had to be very carefully held in place while the heads were mounted and torqued down. Without factory torque specifications, we followed a torque chart based on bolt sizes, beginning in the center of the head and working crosswise alternately, towards the front and back of the heads. We began breaking this engine in by running it stationary, with a jury-rigged oil gauge and a big fan in front of the radiator. When it got hot, it started leaking water. We torqued it down again, and repeated the process. Not until there were no more leaks did I begin driving the car. It would spring a small head-gasket leak and I would re-torque the head bolts again. We had to assume that any water leak might be getting into the oil, so each time there was a leak, we had to dump the oil and change the filters until finally, after it had been driven about 300 miles, the gaskets quit leaking. Even though we didn't fill the twelve-quart sump each time, we still went through several cases of oil. A little advice from the factory would have helped a lot!

It was obvious that these engines were designed for quick pit stop service access, with everything right on top of the engine. The carburetor jets were quick and easy to change although the spark plugs, mounted between the cam covers, were difficult. There were two horizontal Marelli distributors and two Fispa mechanical fuel pumps, one for each bank of six cylinders. A large aluminum oil filler tube with a big coarse-thread screw cap was positioned on each side of the engine so that oil could be added on either or both sides. The battery could be replaced quickly. The generator rested on an aluminum cradle that was part of the large chain case casting, which also housed the water and oil pumps. The generator was driven by a coupling and could be removed quickly by loosening a clamp strap.

These small-displacement twelve cylinder engines were very efficient for 1953. The number 250 represents the metric displacement of each cylinder, multiplied by twelve cylinders for a total of three liters, which equates to only 186 cubic inches, tiny by comparison to the typical American engines of the same period. However, with only 9:1 compression ratio and just two valves per cylinder and hemispherical combustion chambers, they produced 240 horsepower at 7200 rpm with normal aspiration. That amounts to eighty horsepower per liter. They had twelve intake and exhaust ports for straight-through breathing. A single camshaft for each bank operated six rockers mounted on a common shaft with needle-bearing rollers, to minimize friction. The hardened rocker tips worked directly on the valve stems. The bronze valve guides had a spiral oil groove to ensure valve-stem lubrication. Without seals, the guides were designed to allow a bit of oil through. It was not enough to smoke when the engine was running, but when the engine was shut off a small amount of oil would drain down these guides, into the combustion chambers, so the engine smoked when first started, but cleared up quickly. If first-time buyers didn't know this they would assume the engine was using oil.

Having nothing to guide me, I decided to color-code the oil, fuel and water lines as was done on ships I had worked on during the war. I painted the chassis frame red, the sprung suspension parts gray and the hydraulic dampers and oil lines yellow. The huge four-choke Weber carburetors

The restored, running engine with three four-choke Weber carburetors.

dominated the engine bay. In the accompanying photograph, note the round tube stub just above the front edge of the tire below the Fispa fuel pump. The body was welded to the tubular frame with several of these tubes on each side of the frame. Ron cut these to remove the body in order to work on the body and the chassis separately. He made press-fit tube sleeves, with hardened pull-pins that would enable quick installation and easy removal of the body in the future. We thought the chassis was so interesting that it might be desirable to show it without the body at a car show, and in fact, Kirk White did display it that way at the 1969 New York Auto Show.

Warren Fitzgerald wrote that the 250MM has more of a "nervous system" than a throttle response! John Bond, publisher of *Road & Track*, after testing Phil Hill's 250MM, wrote, "Never in my life have I accelerated so rapidly, traveled so fast, or decelerated so suddenly." It was the fastest car they had ever tested up to that time, recording zero-to-sixty in 4.9 seconds! I took this car to the state highway truck scales, and as I recall, with gas and oil, it weighed less than 2000 pounds.

With the three four-choke Webers, each choke was feeding one cylinder directly down the manifold, into the hemispherical combustion chamber, and was then exhausted through its individual exhaust pipe. Those engines could breathe! And the torque just kept coming on almost to the engine's redline. It was *fast!* Phil Hill established his reputation as a first rank driver racing a 250MM Barchetta very successfully in California.

Some writers had stated that these early Ferraris were a handful to handle compared to other competition cars of the same era. I never thought so, but then I certainly never drove them to their limit, nor did I have the opportunity to compare them to other competition cars of the same era. They had a multiple disc clutch that was either in or out. You did not slip the clutch—for fear of warping the plates. You let the clutch engage quickly, with just enough throttle to avoid killing the engine, then you hit the throttle. It did take some practice, but once the clutch was engaged, it ran like a scared rabbit. The brakes had big, steel liners shrunk into finned aluminum drums to dissipate the heat. Independent front suspension was by a transverse leaf spring, with a live rear axle with leaf springs, traction bars and hydraulic Houdaille dampers all around. Ferrari was one of the last race car manufacturers to adopt disk brakes. As far as I was concerned, they drove just great!

I sold this car in 1969, together with my 8C-2900 B Alfa Romeo and a 1956 Ferrari GT, with a low-roof Boano body, to Kirk White, a dealer in Pennsylvania. I got $12,000 for the 250MM Ferrari, $14,000 for the 2.9 Alfa and $10,700 for the Boano. I took a very nice Gullwing Mercedes in

The finished 250MM Ferrari Barchetta #0336.

trade for $7,800. On today's market a 250MM Ferrari Barchetta is worth about $1.6 million! We must remember, however, that when I sold these cars, I got all they were worth, and I usually made a profit. In a recent e-mail, Kirk white said, "Wouldn't it have been clever of us to have never sold either of those wonderful cars?"

When we delivered these three cars across town to an open car carrier, I drove the Alfa and let our son Brian, who was a senior in high school at the time, drive the 250MM Ferrari. I usually let him drive some of these exotic cars just enough to learn firsthand what they were like. When he was late getting to the truck, I was worried that he might have had a problem and I was about to go back to look for him when he came around the corner. It seems that Brian just couldn't resist driving around the high school a couple of times on his way to meet me.

I wouldn't let the truck driver take the 250MM to the top ramp of his open carrier because I was afraid he would warp the clutch plates. I took it up myself. I had to get a pretty good run at it to keep from killing the engine, and then jam on the brakes when I got to the top to keep from going too far. I took about three runs at it, but I finally made it! Today, huge fleets of enclosed transport carriers, with hydraulic lift-gates to load their precious cargo, are kept busy year-round transporting and pampering these valuable automobiles all over America.

One can imagine my surprise when, in 1970, Dick Merritt, co-author of the Ferrari book I had so admired, showed up at my business wanting to sell me a wrecked 1953 Ferrari 250MM competition Barchetta (small boat), #0390MM. He had heard from someone that I was crazy enough to tackle the restoration of a basket case foreign sports-racing car. And he had a real basket case in his trailer. He bought the car from Tom Oleson, a racecar mechanic from Salt Lake City. Dick said Oleson was towing this Ferrari in an enclosed trailer from California in the wintertime, and the trailer had gone over the bank into a river. The very lightweight aluminum

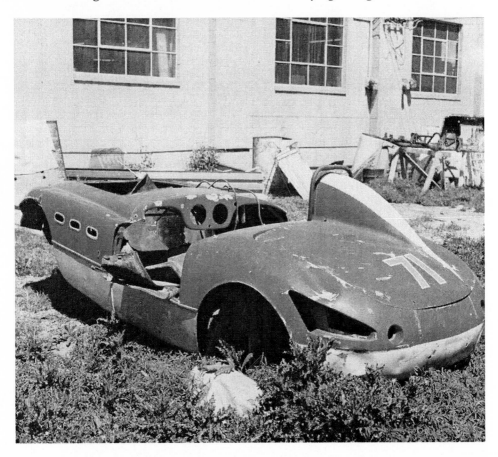

#0390MM 250MM Ferrari Barchetta as purchased from Dick Merritt.

body was badly crumpled. These early Ferraris had a very strong, rigid oval tubular frame, so banging around in the trailer as it went into the river had not damaged the frame at all. The aluminum body was formed over a very lightweight, round steel tube framework. The body was bent up pretty badly, especially in the nose.

To make matters worse, Dick told us the engine had been allowed to freeze. The aluminum block was cracked down the center of each bank, between several of the pressed-in steel cylinder liners, and the aluminum heads were also cracked between valve seats, so compared to the engine, fixing the body was not much of a problem for Ron.

Going over the bank into the river didn't help the body much.

The dismantled engine, transmission and about a million small pieces were in boxes of all sizes. Dick wanted $4,000 for it. He guaranteed it was all there, and that if anything was missing he would provide whatever I needed if I wanted to tackle the restoration of such a basket case. Dick said he had several Ferrari engines in his basement. Having just sold 0336MM I wanted another Ferrari competition sports car. By this time, I felt that Ron could work miracles, and that I had learned enough about finding rare parts and service sources, so I took a chance and bought it.

The first order of business was for Ron to finish dismantling the engine to see how extensive the damage was. The cracking of the block was not really bad as it was merely in the water jackets that were not stressed. The sign business requires expert aluminum welding and Ron was a master

The finished engine bay is dominated by the huge carburetors.

Ferrari Barchetta #0390MM after the restoration.

welder. He first machined a solid steel mandrel to bolt into the main bearing journals to hold the block true, and he did the same for the camshaft journals to hold the heads true. He then ground into the cracks to form a channel into which he would do a substantial weld, then one at a time, he heated the block and heads to about 400 degrees in our big oven we used for vacuum forming acrylic plastic. While they were hot, he TIG-welded the cracks, then put them back in the oven, heated them again to relieve any stresses, and let them slowly cool in the oven overnight. This process was repeated several times over several days. There was no distortion whatsoever. He ground the welds perfectly smooth so the gaskets would seat properly. The welding was so good that I had no doubts that the engine would perform as good as new. Moreover, it was unlikely the engine would ever be highly stressed again. Because of the frost damage done to the

Another historical competition Ferrari saved from oblivion!

engine, I took the opportunity to buy another Ferrari 250MM, chassis #0330, from Tom Oleson. It had no body, and Tom Caulfield had the engine. I bought them to use as a backup parts chassis to #0390MM, but because the 0330MM engine had never been damaged we rebuilt it with all new factory parts. I was now able to get parts from Luigi Chinetti and Bill Harrah's dealerships after sending photographs and explaining what we were doing with these cars.

I decided to personally rebuild this third engine, #0330. I had learned from George Pradervand that the Ferrari factory race team mechanics set the valve timing for *each valve*, using a dial indicator on top of the valve rockers, to begin opening the valve corresponding to the flywheel degree marks. Previously, we had set the valve clearances for number one and number six cylinders of the V-12 engine and then just set the specified clearances on the rest of the valves.

I had read about cars having problems with fuel starvation caused by centrifugal force sloshing the fuel to one side on long curves. This would result in the engine cutting out, and sometimes burning the valves. I noted that these carburetors had small, separate canister reservoirs on each side of each carburetor, so that fuel would drain back into the accelerator pump chamber on hard cornering. When I first fired-up this engine, I could not believe how much more responsive it was than the first two engines because of the more precise valve adjustment. It really wanted to run! This is an example of how and why race team mechanics are able to do things ordinary mechanics do not do. George Pradervand was also the fastest mechanic I ever saw. He had learned every trick, every shortcut, working in the pits where seconds counted.

We put engine #0330 in the restored 0390MM chassis. When we sandblasted the chassis, besides 0330MM we found a second chassis number, 0276MM, raising the question that this may have been an earlier factory team car that had been rebuilt and renumbered by the factory, which they occasionally did. At the time we were doing all this restoration work the numbers were not as important as they have since become. Today, their early racing history, progression of owners, restorations and body changes are all tracked and recorded by their chassis numbers. We restored all three of these 250MM chassis alike, with the color-coding of the frame, suspension, fluid lines and the red crinkle-lacquered heads with the paint filed off the "Ferrari" logo.

In 1971 I sold the second 250 Ferrari # 0390MM to Peter Giddings for $18,000. Grand Prix racing had recently begun in America and vintage car racing was being promoted as a preliminary event to the Grand Prix. The crowds loved to see and hear the old racecars run. My wife and I, with Tom Haynie and our daughter Barbara, attended the Grand Prix at Watkins Glen and saw Peter Giddings drive the 250MM in the preliminaries.

Peter Giddings also later bought chassis #0330MM (now with the rebuilt engine #0390MM) as a backup to chassis #0390MM. He eventually sold #0330MM to Rudy Pas of the Netherlands, who fitted another Barchetta body. It was then sold to Art Valdez in 1987, who raced it extensively in vintage race events. In fact, Valdez drove the car in the Mille Miglia in Italy *five times* and as far as I know he never had any problems with the engine that was saved by Ron's expert welding.

Testing 0336MM on Christmas day with a frozen Tom Haynie.

Every time I started one of these engines, I knew I was in for a thrill. When we finished the first Ferrari, #0336MM, even before Ron made the new fold-down windshield, I took Tom Haynie for a fast, cold ride on Christmas day in 1970. A neighbor snapped the accompanying picture as we turned into our driveway. Tom was both thrilled and frozen! Of all the sports cars I have ever owned, these 250MM Ferraris and the 8C-2300 Alfa Romeos are my favorites.

Looking back on these 250MMs, it is amazing that we restored three of them. Only seventeen 250MMs were built, of which only thirteen were Barchettas! Today, each one of these Barchettas would be worth about $1,600,000.

6

The 1959 410 Superamerica Ferrari

When, to support his racing passion, Enzo Ferrari began building road cars to sell to the public, he found a ready market among the world's most affluent people. His early production was very limited and the best of the Italian carrozzerie (body designers/manufacturers) were anxious to clothe these beautifully engineered masterpieces with equally beautiful bodies. Battista Pinin Farina, who later changed his professional name to Pininfarina in 1961, was one of the best and justifiably most proud carrozzerie. These Italian body designers were artists also, and some were as proud of their work and just as aloof as Enzo Ferrari. The story has been told that when Ferrari and Pininfarina, both strong-willed men, had to meet to discuss a contract for bodies, neither man was willing to go the other's office, so they compromised by meeting halfway, for a luncheon meeting. These men had known each other for years, but they were a lot like Hollywood movie moguls saying "I'll have my people call your people and we'll do lunch."

In any event, this meeting resulted in some of the most beautiful and exciting gran turismo automobiles that were ever built. In 1955, Ferrari introduced the 410 Superamerica, a flagship model that sold for about $19,000, at a time when a "regular" 250 GT Ferrari cost "only" about $12,000. The most expensive car produced in America at that time was the Lincoln Continental Mark II, priced a little less than $10,000. The 410 Superamerica had the larger 4.9-liter (305 cubic inch) racing engine designed by Aurelio Lampredi that, even detuned for the street, produced

340 horsepower. The Series III engines had minor changes and produced 360 horsepower at 7000 rpm. The 410 Superamerica, fitted with custom-built bodies, set new automotive design standards that were emulated by other automobile manufacturers for years to come. Detroit designers used many design cues from these Italian carrozzerie that could be seen years afterwards on American cars. The 410 Superamerica was built in three series. Only about fifteen Series I, eight Series II and fifteen Series II were built, making them very rare and exclusive even when new. They had all the requisites to become coveted collectibles. Because they were so expensive almost all of then had prominent or famous original owners, another factor that, for some collectors, adds value as a collectible. Movie and recording stars, European royalty, and very rich oil sheiks were among those that bought them.

When you are involved in restoring old cars, you very seldom have any good luck. There's lots of bad news, but good news is scarce. This was the one time I had some good luck. In 1969 I got wind of one of the last 1959 Series III 410 Superamericas in New Jersey that was priced very low because it had been abused and poorly maintained. It was running very badly with a cloud of smoke trailing behind, indicative of very serious engine problems. After several phone calls and getting photographs I decided to buy it to restore and sent one of my employees with my truck to pick it up. When it arrived in Fort Collins, I was pleased to see the body had never been damaged and the glass and instrument panel were in good condition. The leather was dry and cracked, the carpets were dirty and worn, the paint was dull, the engine compartment was dirty and it did, indeed, lay down a virtual smoke screen when it ran. I knew that the Ferrari engines of that era had no valve guide seals, and that they smoked when first started but quickly cleared up. This one did not clear up. In fact it got worse. It also rode rough. I assumed there were broken piston rings or a holed piston, and perhaps broken coil springs or shock absorbers.

I drove the car to Boulder to my friend, George Pradervand, the ex–Ferrari pit-crew mechanic from Switzerland. The car would run strongly at first, then begin missing and running very poorly. George did a compression check, and it was OK. He pulled the cam-covers and the pan, but could find nothing wrong. But the engine still would not run right. I decided that if we had to rebuild the engine I would do it in my own shop, and I drove the car back to Fort Collins and parked it. I wanted to think about this puzzle for a while.

Over the years I had gotten pretty good at diagnosing car problems. I had learned to always look for the fundamentals first. If this engine had good compression, it had good rings, good valves and no broken pistons.

The oil pressure was very good. I got to thinking about the valve design, which allows a little oil from the camshaft to drain back into the combustion chambers through the valve guides after the engine shuts off, while the larger part of the oil in the cam boxes drains through the drain gallery to the sump. I thought, what if something is plugged up, preventing the oil from draining back into the sump while the car is running, and the oil pressure is filling the cam boxes with oil and forcing it down the guides into the combustion chamber? That would foul the spark plugs, causing it to misfire and also explaining the smoking.

Next morning, I had Ron Kerr pull the external oil pipes that drain the oil from the cam boxes back into the sump. Unlike the smaller Colombo engines, which had internal oil passages, the Lampredi engines had external oil pipes. Sure enough, the oil return pipes were almost completely blocked with sludge! Ron cleaned all these pipes, installed them with new gaskets, and the engine ran fine! This meant that we had lucked out. I had bought this car very cheaply because it was assumed the engine had serious problems, but by looking for simple problems we cured the engine problem with an hour's work.

We installed new oil filters and flushed the engine with 10-weight oil and kerosene by running it at a fast idle for about thirty minutes, then draining it and changing the filters. We did this about three times, then filled it with the prescribed Castrol oil. I took the car out on the road—and it *ran*! This car had great gobs of power and torque. I had no doubt it would do the reputed 160 mph.

I took the car to a local shock absorber shop we used and had the mechanics lift the car so I could inspect the suspension system with them. I could see that the frame was still the familiar oval tube chassis frame. It had new A-arm independent front suspension with coil springs and tubular shocks, but the rear suspension was still a live axle with trailing arms and leaf springs. I had the mechanics disconnect and test the shocks, all of which proved in good condition. We checked all the ball joints and

The rare 1959 410 Superamerica Ferrari with Pininfarina body.

steering linkage and found them all tight. So what was causing the rough ride and erratic steering? I checked the tires and only then noted that someone had fitted cheap bias-ply tires. I had a new set of Pirelli radials fitted and the wheels balanced. I could not believe the difference! All the harshness and squirrelly steering was gone. This car now drove and handled like a good Ferrari should. All that remained to be done was cosmetic, the easy part.

Rather than repaint the car, which still had its original paint, I sent it to a good detail shop. For a couple hundred dollars they cleaned and detailed the engine compartment and buffed, polished and waxed the car and polished what little chrome there was.

We then sent the car to our upholsterer for all new leather trim with Bridge of Weir leather that was a close match to the original color. I had them make new Wilton wool carpets bound in the same leather, and they shampooed the vinyl headliner. While the car was not cosmetically like new, it was very, very nice and a thoroughly good driving Ferrari. I was told that there were only two bodies like this and the other one belonged to Bill Harrah of casino fame, who was also the western states Ferrari dealer.

To appreciate how good this body design was one has to remember the huge tailfins and massive chrome being used on American cars at that

The restored leather interior—note the left-hand drive built for export.

All sorted out—a beautiful, fast Gran Turismo automobile.

time. This car was larger and heavier than any previous Ferrari I had owned. It had more passenger and luggage space and for 1960 it offered state-of-the-art luxury grand touring in the European manner. It was extremely powerful, but not really as quick, in terms of acceleration, as the smaller 250 MM competition Ferraris were.

I drove the car for a while, and was satisfied with myself for solving most of its problems by using common sense. I had not spent much money on it either, and made a very nice profit when I sold it. Unfortunately, I no longer have my records of this car, and do not have the serial number, and I don't recall who bought it or what I sold it for. Only thirty-seven 410 Superamericas were built. Today, because of its rarity and especially the custom body style, it would undoubtedly now have sparkling new or rebuilt Borrani wire wheel "jewelry" and a high-dollar paint job, and probably another new leather interior, and be worth about $900,000 in show condition.

As the name implies, these cars were aimed squarely at the U.S. market. Luigi Chinetti was still the sole U.S. importer, and his son, Coco, was by then involved in the business. They were treating the customers a little better now. I had read so much about Luigi Chinetti, how he had won Le Mans three or four times, first driving 8C-2.3 Alfa Romeos, then Ferrari. He had to leave Italy because he detested Mussolini when that was not good for one's health. He first went to France then fled to America, where he worked in New York City tuning Rolls-Royce automobiles. Some wag speculated that those were the quickest Rolls-Royces to be found anywhere.

On a trip back east, I got up enough nerve to try to talk to Chinetti at his facility, which was by then in Connecticut. I came armed with photos of my 8C Alfa and my 250 MM Ferraris hoping they would break the ice. I was surprised when he asked me into his office, and he was very friendly when I explained how much I loved the old Alfas and early Ferraris. He showed me around their rather small facility, but, not wanting to impose on his hospitality, I did not stay long. But when I was ready to leave, he asked me to wait a moment. He came back with two out-of-print Ferrari yearbooks which he had autographed, with an inscription saying he had won the 24 Hours of Le Mans in 1932, 1934, and 1949. I found him to be very kind and friendly. Perhaps I had touched his soft spot with my pictures of his two beloved makes of cars—or maybe he was just mellowing with age.

7

The Lusso Berlinetta Ferraris

Every time I read a new Ferrari road test in *Road & Track*, full of praise for the great road cars Ferrari was building by this time, I wanted one as a personal car to drive, at least for a while. I wanted one that I knew to be in very good mechanical condition. I had corresponded with Massimo Colombo in Italy, who had helped me with getting parts from the factory. Knowing he had a good reputation among many European and American car people, I bought, sight unseen, a used 1964 Ferrari Lusso Berlinetta that he had just rebuilt in Italy. I knew there could be a risk in doing this, but when the car came by container into the Port of Los Angeles, and I flew out to drive it home, I was pleased with it. The Lusso (luxurious) had the same three-liter Gioacchino Colombo designed engine that the 250 MM had, although it was by then somewhat updated, and with just three two-choke Webers it developed 265 hp, as I recall, and still redlined at 7200 rpm. By now the Ferraris were fitted with a conventional Borg & Beck clutch, which was quite light to operate and smooth to engage. It still had the same four-speed transmission that had a reputation of wearing out the synchro rings rather rapidly if the transmission was not allowed to warm up before any aggressive driving began.

Because it was in a container, I did not have to uncrate it, as I did the 2.9 Alfa (the subject of the following chapter). After I let the electric fuel pump run to fill the carburetors, it fired right up. Only one gallon of gas was allowed on cars being shipped by sea, so I filled it at the first station I saw. Before leaving California, I drove up to Vandenberg Air Force base to visit our oldest daughter Robin and her husband Fred Foss, who was a meteorologist there. We had dinner at a fine seafood restaurant on the pier at Santa Barbara. That was the best (and last) abalone I ever had! Even though I was not going really fast and was watching for patrol cars, I got a ticket near Barstow before I was even out of California! That cop must have been hiding behind a big saguaro cactus.

I thought I was really in tall cotton, though, driving this red Ferrari across Arizona and New Mexico at about 100 miles an hour until I saw an old beat-up, rusted out Buick Roadmaster, slowly coming up in my rear view mirror. It took him a long time, but he finally passed, doing about 110, and as he did I noted it was a young guy in an Army uniform, perhaps going back to camp after a leave. As he went by, I noted a Georgia license plate on the car, and thought to myself that he'll never make it, driving that beater that fast. I passed him when he stopped for gas and over the next couple hundred miles we passed each other two or three times until I turned north at Albuquerque, for home. As I did so, I felt sorry for him in that old clunker, obviously in a real big hurry to get wherever he was going. I hoped it didn't fall apart on him.

Not long after crossing into Colorado, near Walsenburg, I was doing about 100, when I suddenly heard this very fast clicking sound, and thought it was a rod bearing going out! I cut the ignition, depressed the clutch and coasted down a long grade to a stop. I carefully touched the starter button, but the engine was jammed! As I sat there, with my Ferrari induced arrogance slowly deflating, I started to laugh. I thought about that soldier, who was probably still going down the highway at about 110 miles an hour,

The 1964 Ferrari Lusso Berlinetta imported from Italy.

with that beat-up old Buick floating up and down on its Detroit suspension, and here I was with my fancy imported Ferrari broken down by the side of the road.

Fortunately, I had rolled to a stop just a couple of blocks from a large service station and nice motel across the divided highway. I walked over and had them tow the car to the motel where I checked in for the night. I called my friend George Pradervand, my very talented Swiss immigrant Ferrari racing team mechanic. I had recently co-signed his note to help him arrange a bank loan to open his own garage in Boulder. He dropped everything to come pick me up the next morning with his trailer. After taking me home in Fort Collins, he took the car back to his garage in Boulder. After removing the pan, he found nothing wrong with the rod or main bearings, which was a big relief. However, he had to remove the chain cover in front of the engine to remove the heads to get to the valves. He eventually found a small nut that had vibrated loose from one of the carburetor chokes, and the nut was inhaled. It had jammed between a valve and the seat but had done no serious damage. He only had to re-seat and adjust the valve, and it was fine.

After keeping the car for a while and thoroughly enjoying it, I sold it to get something else. I don't remember to whom I sold that Ferrari, nor do I have the serial number.

A couple years later I had another opportunity to own a Lusso Ferrari, almost by accident. At that time my company had a sales and service office in Boulder. I was there frequently and usually went by the Sports Car Center where I had first drooled over the XK-E's, the new Alfas and the usual gaggle of British sports cars. That is also where I first met George Pradervand, working on a damaged Ferrari 250GT. There were a few Ferraris around by then, some owned by kids from all over the country whose very wealthy families sent them to the University of Colorado in Boulder.

Dabney Collins, a sometimes semi-professional Ferrari driver and full time machinist, lived in Boulder and helped me out a few times when I was over my head with something. Word got around that I bought cars from time to time. One day, a young man called me who wanted to sell his 1962 short wheelbase Ferrari 250GT Berlinetta. He wanted $6,000 for it. He brought it to my home for me to see and drive. It was very nice cosmetically, and of course it was blindingly fast since it was a competition car, but it was also rough riding at street speed and the interior was devoid of all but the essential trim. I thought the price was too high and I turned it down. Today that car would be worth $1,800,000 if it had a steel body, and about $4,500,000 if the body was aluminum. I wasn't interested enough to find out what the body metal was.

Jim Kahan, an engineer in Denver, called me in 1971, wanting to sell his 1965 Lusso Berlinetta that he had bought new. He was having trouble getting it to run properly. There was no Colorado dealer then and his neighborhood mechanic was almost afraid to touch the car. By now, a new Ferrari cost around $14,000 and this car had very low mileage on it. I went to see and drive it. There really wasn't much wrong with it, but it was definitely not running like a Ferrari. The carburetors would spit-back, then it would run properly for a while, then act up again. I told Jim that I didn't think there was much wrong with the car, that it acted like it was fuel starvation, and would be easy to sort out. He still wanted to sell the car, so I bought it for $5,000.

By this time, I was very familiar with the 250 Ferrari engines, and had learned a lot about Weber carburetors. Driving the car home, I was convinced it was a fuel problem, and sure enough, after rebuilding the mechanical fuel pump, installing a new electrical pump, and installing new fuel filters the engine ran fine, with no hesitation at all, but it still lacked power. Some of the nuts holding the carburetors down on the manifold

Balancing the six Weber carburetor venturi chokes with a Unison gauge.

The 1965 Lusso Berlinetta.

are hard to reach and I suspected the three twin-choke carburetors might be sucking air at their base mounting to the manifold that made the mixture too lean. Sure enough, some of the nuts were so loose I could almost turn them with my fingers. Jim's mechanic may never have thought of them or that anything that simple would be such a large part of the car's problems. I had made a special wrench just for this purpose, and when they were properly tightened, with lock washers, the car ran like a Ferrari should.

This was a lovely car to drive. A number of books and articles had given the impression that these early twelve cylinder Ferraris were temperamental and difficult to keep in tune. I never found that to be true. I knew that Ferrari could not have won so many races with cars that were either fragile or unreliable. I also knew that, in those days, the engines and chassis under these beautiful bodies were merely de-tuned versions of the racing machines. I had read that Luigi Chinetti told his rich clientele who bought his street machines to "keep your gold-plated screwdrivers out of the works and your car will not give you trouble." I'm sure he especially meant the carburetors and distributors. I found that once properly adjusted, these cars were extremely reliable, tractable, strong and trouble-free. Admittedly, they liked to run, and were somewhat unhappy and unpleasant to drive in slow traffic. These cars should be driven at least enough to bring the entire drive-train up to operating temperature, which took at least twenty miles, not less than once a month. Too many Ferraris sit around without being driven enough. They are just beginning to run at our U.S. speed limits. Mine seemed to be most happy at about 90 miles an hour

The Ferrari 250 Lusso GT engine bay.

and more. I had noted that every car I drove seemed to run best and more efficiently somewhere near its torque peak rpm range. On a '60s-era Ferrari, that was about 110 mph, but driving with one eye on the road and the other on the rear view mirror took much of the pleasure out of driving a fast car on the highway. And it didn't help much if they were red! At least this Lusso Ferrari wasn't red, so I didn't get as many tickets with it as I had with the red one.

I'm reminded of an incident when the U.S. speed limit was 55 miles an hour. Jackie and I were coming back to Colorado from California in my Mercedes sedan. We were on a long, open stretch of highway in New Mexico and I was driving about 70, keeping an eye out front and back for a highway patrol car. I could see for fifty miles in all directions, but out of nowhere, here came one, flashing his lights. When I pulled over, he said I was going seventy. I didn't argue, but while he was writing the ticket, I told him that if I had to cross the United States at 55 miles an hour, I couldn't do it. Even if I knew I would be caught and the penalty was death I still couldn't do it. It didn't help but at least it made him smile while he finished writing the ticket.

This was basically the same Colombo-designed engine as the 1953

250MM engine, but with some changes made from time to time by the factory. The plugs were now on the outside, making them easier to change. The distributors were larger, and were now mounted vertically at the back of the engine, with two sets of points each; thus each set of points fired three cylinders, and were therefore less prone to misfire at high rpm.

The twin spin-on oil filters were a big improvement, and the correct ones had check-valves to prevent oil spill when removing them. The twin oil filler caps remained on each side of the engine, but now up front. Also prominent under the hood were big adjustable tube shocks and three twin-choke Weber carburetors, with large housings for three big round air filters. They were much better filters, but they hid a good part of the beautiful engine. I fitted velocity stacks, with fine mesh screens, to this car to run it without the big air filter because I wanted to see the beautiful engine better. The Lusso also had a belt-driven fan.

In 1968 I built a new home with an oversized garage that had a pit that was normally kept covered. I could remove the cover, drive over the pit, and change the oil or work on the undercarriage of my cars at home on the weekend. I enjoyed tuning them and getting them to run like they should, as I did with this Lusso.

I drove the Lusso for about nine months, then sold it to a United Airlines captain for $7,500, making about $2,000 for no more than a tune-up. Nowadays, when I read how much a Ferrari dealer charges for a tune-up on these early street Ferraris, I can only assume they must have an awful lot of overhead.

In the late 1970s I bought a 1967 330 GTC from Pete Civati that had been owned by John Frankenheimer, the director of the movie *Grand Prix*. Jackie and I drove it to Astoria, Oregon, and I found it to be a delightful car if you could drive it fast enough. It was awful in town. The steering was ungodly heavy for parking and it was terrible in traffic. But if you could turn it loose a bit, it loved to run at 90 to 110 mph. Jackie was constantly telling me to slow down. Interstate 84 had recently been completed, and driving from Boise to Portland at those speeds was a delight. As it happened, I had to fly back to Denver for an important meeting and Jackie was to drive the Ferrari back to Boise where I would fly to meet her. Now, Jackie is a bit uneasy when she is the passenger at high speed, but the first thing she said when I met her was that I was right—the 330 GT was most happy at 110 mph. In fact, even though we both left about the same time, she from Portland, me from downtown Denver, by the time I went through the rigmarole of getting to the airports and flying with the usual delays, I beat her to the Boise airport by just an hour! This just shows what automobile travel could be like on our beautiful wide-open interstate highways in the west with a good fast car and no speed limits.

Then in the late 1990s, I owned a 1985 400i Ferrari for a short time. To me, it was a less interesting car than the 1960s coupes. With all the power controls and electronics it was not much different from any good upscale car except for one thing—it still drove like only a Ferrari can. But in my view the Lusso Berlinettas were the best looking and the sweetest driving street Ferraris I ever owned. And they were still simple enough that I could tune and take care of them myself. The market has been recognizing this recently.

Today, each of these 250 GT Lusso Berlinettas is worth $500,000.

8

The Maharajah's 2.9 Alfa Romeo

Keeping Ron busy restoring nothing but Alfa Romeos was proving to be impossible. I was continually inquiring of a number of overseas Alfa owners who might be willing to sell their cars. Mr. J. H. Jarvis of Adelaide, Australia, had several Alfas but wouldn't sell his 8C 2.3 cars. However, he had a rare 1938 short-chassis 8C-2900B Touring bodied Alfa Romeo roadster that he was willing to sell. When the Grand Prix formula was changed, after the 1936 season as I recall, supercharged engines were no longer allowed and the factory was stuck with about fifty very expensive engines and transaxles.

These straight eight double overhead-cam supercharged engines were a further development of Vittorio Jano's 2.3 liter engine design. They still had the central gear-tower that powered everything. By then the engine had two small Roots-type superchargers, with pop-off valves, one on each side of the central gear tower. They were now mounted low on the left side of the engine instead of the right side as before. Two Weber carburetors were fitted, one on each end of the twin blower, each feeding four cylinders through separate finned aluminum manifolds. The de Dion transaxles were an all-new design for an Alfa sports car, with independent suspension on the rear wheels. The factory decided they would utilize these engines and transaxles to built forty-some of these very extraordinary and exclusive cars. Capable of 118 to 140 miles per hour depending on their gearing, they were advertised as the fastest sports cars in the world in 1938. They were also the most expensive sports cars in the world, costing about $19,000

The 1938 8C-2900 B Alfa with Superleggera (light-weight) Touring body.

As it came from Australia. Chassis no. 412019, engine no. 422018.

($262,000 in 2005 dollars). With these detuned Grand Prix engines and transaxles, they were very advanced, with four-wheel independent suspension and huge finned hydraulic brakes. They had custom-built two-seater envelope bodies. Most of them were sold to royalty or extremely wealthy people. After considerable correspondence and photographs from Mr.

Mr. and Mrs. Scherr crossing the ramp at Pebble Beach, August 2005.

Jarvis, I bought his car sight unseen, for U.S. $10,000, FOB Adelaide, Australia, in 1969.

It's hard to believe now, but at that time, Alfa enthusiasts considered these 2.9 Alfas less desirable than the older 8C 2.3's, especially the bored-out 2.6 liter racing Monzas. I flew to San Francisco and got the car released from Customs. The car came in a fantastic solid wood crate. I think that crate alone would cost as much today as I paid for the car then! I hired two stevedores to uncrate the car. My brother Walter, who had brought a trailer up from Santa Ana, and I loaded the car onto his open trailer and we wrapped it in heavy plastic to protect it in case of rain. We started for Colorado with it on the trailer but about halfway home, I found that the plastic cover was rubbing the paint badly so I decided to drive it the rest of the way while Walter followed with the trailer. I went over 10,650 foot high Wolf Creek Pass in southern Colorado like a banshee, passing everything on the road.

My trip home with this car is more fully and better described in Simon Moore's definitive book, *The Immortal 2.9 Alfa Romeo*. It was originally sold, through his personal agent, to the Maharajah of Indore, believed to be the seventh or eighth richest man in the world at that time. And he bought two of them! Mine was reputedly intended for the Maharini. It still had less than 10,000 miles on the odometer when I got it.

These cars had dry-sump lubrication with a 4.5 gallon oil tank, filled from inside the trunk. When I reached Pueblo, it occurred to me to check the oil in the trunk. I was amazed to find that it had used most of that oil in the thousand miles I drove it home, yet never fouled the plugs! Keith Hellon, who had experience with the 2.9 engines, suggested that the seals in the blower were probably dried out from lack of use, allowing the blower to suck oil from the drive gears. The car was, of course, much more powerful and faster than my 8C 2.3 Alfa and was superior in most every way, yet I too preferred the aesthetics of the open-fender body style of the older cars and their more "lively" nature when driving them. In the 2.9 the driver is much more insulated from the sounds, sight and feel of the road. The difference is somewhat like flying a modern Cessna compared to an open cockpit airplane. I only kept the car about a year, long enough to learn all about it and to drive it quite a bit in our open countryside. I sold it in December 1970 to Kirk White in Pennsylvania, together with my first 250 MM Ferrari and a 1956 Ferrari Boano GT that we had just restored.

For all three cars I got $29,000 and a really gorgeous 1957 Gullwing Mercedes that Kirk had at the time. With $14,000 of that deal coming for the 2.9 Alfa, I made 40 percent on my investment after satisfying my curiosity as to what it was like to drive one of the most exclusive and expensive sports cars ever built.

Kirk sold the car to Edmond Osborn in Ohio, who discovered a crack in the blower casing, which might have explained the loss of oil. He repaired it, and in the ensuing ten years raced the car at Mosport, Watkins Glen and Nelson Ledges. He also showed the car at times. In 1979 he sold it to Bill Serri, who had another of the 2.9s. Bill sold it to Tom Perkins, who kept the car for several years. Phil Reilly finally restored the car for Tom Perkins. It was repainted a soft cream color with red leather interior. They made new rear fender skirts to replace the missing originals.

Tom Perkins sold the car to Ralph Lauren, who showed the car at Pebble Beach, then sold it to Ray Scherr, the present owner. It has been repainted again and took first in class at Pebble Beach in August 2005.

The current Sports Car Market Price Guide *values the short-chassis 8C-2900 roadsters at $8–$10 million. The 8C 2.9 Alfa is undoubtedly the most valuable of all the cars I ever owned.*

9

The 1922 Targa Florio Mercedes

In the spring of 1974 Ron Kerr was offered a better position with Teledyne Water-Pic Company in Fort Collins, as a prototype fabricator. Gene Rouse and I were among the seventeen local founders of the Water-Pic Company. We were both officers and directors from its inception in 1961 until we sold the company to Teledyne in 1968. Gene owned a sizeable camera business but sold it to work for Teledyne, and was soon made president of Teledyne Water-Pic. When Gene offered Ron the job I encouraged him to take it, as it would provide much better security and retirement benefits than my small private company could offer. He had worked for me for nineteen years, the last nine spent restoring cars. Not only was Ron a good employee, he was also a good friend. He was an extraordinary, gifted craftsman.

After putting out some feelers, I hired Loran Swanson, who was then working as a gunsmith for a large sporting goods company in Denver. The Army Corps of Engineers trained him as a heavy equipment mechanic and he served in Vietnam in that capacity. He was an expert woodworker, welder, machinist, and metalworker and a good spray painter. He had never restored cars before, but after interviewing him, I knew he had the kind of versatility to do much of the work required. I could tell that he learned things better by observation and hands-on experience than from a textbook. Loran was a bit awed by the fact that his first projects were to be a 1922 Mercedes that Ron had started, a Talbot Lago and a Ferrari that I was planning to buy. But I told him that these cars, after all, were just machines, and he had worked on much more complex military machines in the Army. Loran had some things to learn, but he jumped right in and did just fine. I had never put any time or cost constraints on Ron or Loran when doing a restoration. I wanted everything done the very best we could. Ron was perhaps better at engine work, but Loran was better, perhaps, with transmissions, differentials and machining parts. They were both very versatile craftsmen, which is imperative for a one-man restoration shop.

When Gene Rouse and I visited Vojta Mashek, Vojta told Gene about an interesting 1922 Mercedes racecar that was owned by Mr. Bayard Sheldon, who had brought the car from England in 1962. Gene and I visited Mr. Sheldon at his beautiful country home near Chicago. While we talked to Mr. Sheldon in his family room, a motor-driven wall-to-wall drape was opened to display his lovely big 1929 S Mercedes touring car, through a glass wall. Needless to say, this made a huge, unexpected impression on any guest who had no idea what was behind the tastefully draped wall. In 1967 Gene bought the 1922 Targa Florio Mercedes from Mr. Sheldon and left it with Keith Hellon to restore. At that time, Keith was restoring Alfa Romeos exclusively, but agreed to take the little Mercedes on, to work on it as his other commitments permitted. Progress was very slow because the car had been so extensively modified.

As Germany rose from the ashes of World War I, the financially strapped company turned to racing again as that helped to sell cars. Until 1924, because of war reparations, Germany was barred from the French Grand Prix, still Europe's premier race, so they turned to Voiturette (small car) racing. This led to the design of a totally new family of engines, the first Mercedes designed from the outset to be supercharged. Italy was the first to welcome Mercedes Benz back into competition for the 1922 Targa Florio race through the mountains of Sicily. Mercedes entered two little 1500cc cars. Our subject car was assigned to Minoia, an Italian who had successfully driven a larger Mercedes in the 1921 Targa Florio. For unknown reasons he failed to finish with ignition trouble in the little Mercedes in 1922. Scheef drove the second car and finished twentieth overall.

The car went on to race in many hill climbs and minor events, and probably was driven by young Rudolph Caracciola in 1923 and 1924, for there is a photograph of him in one of the cars. In 1927 the factory sold the car to Raymond Mays, the famous British race driver. He did not intend to race it, wanting instead to convert it to drive on the road. He ordered a sports car body to be built by Corsica, which was only the first of several bodies the car was to carry. It was fitted with a different transmission, smaller wheels and hydraulic brakes, since the original two-wheel brakes had little effect at slowing the car down.

Today, when originality is so important regarding any collectible car's value, we must remember that these now priceless gems were just "used cars" in the 1920s and 1930s, and this was especially true of a racecar that was obsolete. Several subsequent owners in England altered the Mercedes to make it usable as a sports car that could be driven on the street or in amateur racing events. Raymond Mays sold the car to The Hon. Jock Leith (who complained of the brakes), then Captain Fane owned it. He too complained of the brakes and said that his attempt to put four-wheel brakes didn't work because they twisted the front axle and made the car swerve violently!

In 1935 C.W.P. Hampton bought the car, in need of an overhaul, from Jack Bartlett, a London dealer, for about $400. Mr. Hampton registered the car with the EPC-2 plates it still carried when Gene got it. Mr. Hampton mentioned that the rear axle hummed excessively, that the E.N.V. self-change gearbox slipped in some gears and that the brakes hardly worked at all. He had the car completely rebuilt, including hydraulic brakes using a Riley front axle, and with yet another body of his own design and with a new E.N.V. self-change gearbox. With the original high axle ratio it made a very nice looking, fast sports car. This was a lot like what American kids were doing building hotrods.

With the high-speed axle ratio Hampton drove the car at Brooklands in 1939 where it did a standing lap at 80 mph and crossed the line at 100 mph. When Mr. Sheldon brought the car to the United States, he also acquired most of the parts necessary to return the car to its original configuration. This meant building a totally new body, finding correct wheels and tires and a correct transmission, all of which had been changed over time.

Keith Hellon located a Mercedes transmission of the proper type from

The 1922 Targa Florio Mercedes—modified and with a new body.

a 2-liter car, and fitted it to the Targa Florio engine. It was operated with a cone clutch, as I recall. Keith made a good start on the body, but was held up for many reasons. Gene was anxious to get the car finished, so he brought it to Colorado and approached me to finish the car in Fort Collins. I agreed to finish the car at my expense for a half-interest in it. Most of Keith's work was well done, but after we obtained some excellent factory photographs, we had to redo the cockpit part of the body because some of the proportions were wrong. I contacted Marcus Clary, Director of Special Programs for Mercedes Benz of North America. With his help, when the factory museum in Stuttgart realized what we were restoring, they provided the car's total racing history, engine specifications and more excellent photographs from the factory files. Loran stripped it to the bare chassis again. He rebuilt the engine, corrected the body and finished the car in a fairly short time. The toughest parts for us to replicate were the 815 x 105 mm wire wheels with rolled edge rims. I finally found Mr. Elster Hays of Springfield, Ohio, who had the equipment to build six new wheels, using the original splined hubs. I had to order the correct size Dunlop tires and tubes from England.

The engine displaced only 1.5 liters (93 cubic inches). Applying aircraft technology learned during the Great War, it had four cylinders with double overhead cams driven by a vertical gear-driven shaft from the rear of the crankshaft. The cams were ground with an extremely high lift profile operating four valves per cylinder. Watching the valves operate with the engine idling, they closed so fast it was as if they were in a free fall, making a loud click as they closed. The little engine had a vertically mounted Roots type blower, driven off the front of the crankshaft. The engine was

Mercedes supercharged 1.5 liter engine number 55207.

a fixed-head steel block with hemispherical combustion chambers, with separate intake and exhaust ports for each cylinder. Ignition was by an eight-cylinder magneto modified to operate four cylinders. The magneto that came with the car was wrong, and we had to have an eight-cylinder magneto rebuilt so that it fired on every other point. It had a single, updraft carburetor, which made it very hard to start when it was cold, especially before the rings had sealed enough to build compression. The water and oil pumps were also gear-driven. There was no cooling fan. The valves featured flat wafer topped tappets that screwed into hollow valve stems. These were originally designed by Marc Birkigt for Hispano Suiza, and were later used by Alfa Romeo, Ferrari, Lancia and Maserati. These made adjusting the valves precise and extremely simple and easy. A special little tool adjusted the valves one click at a time. By rotating the teeth in the wafers, each click adjusted the clearance exactly one-tenth millimeter. This was a very advanced little Mercedes engine for 1922, and a total departure from Mercedes' large, slow-revving engines of the past. The historical importance of these little engines was not their racing success, but their advanced design, which established a whole new concept in fast, light cars with efficient engine performance. The trend to supercharging became almost universal in the next few years to the extent that almost all Grand Prix cars were supercharged until the Ferrari era began in the closing years of the 1940s.

When the car was finished enough to drive, I drove it in the country and on the streets of Fort Collins sufficiently to begin breaking-in the engine and tuning it. We had retained the hydraulic four-wheel brakes with the Riley front axle that Mr. Hampton had added in 1937. They had

The restored 1922 Targa Florio Mercedes, chassis number 26804.

also made a crossmember for the front ends of the dumbirons that stopped most front-end tramping. I still allowed about an extra block to stop the car. The transmission was an absolute brute! It was non-synchronized, of course, and it sometimes took me so long to find the gear I wanted that the car would almost have come to a stop. The cone clutch that was fitted was not disengaging enough, and Loran had to work on that some more, which helped—but not much. The 1919 Buick we restored was older than this Mercedes but had a three-speed transmission that worked very well compared to this brute. The axle ratio must have been changed at some point because the gearing was quite high, which would have been very unlikely for mountain racing in Sicily. The little car had staggered bucket seats to allow a riding mechanic because the car was not wide enough for two men to sit side-by-side. The car had no mechanical fuel pump. The riding mechanic pressurized the gas tank with a hand-operated air pump, located behind the driver. A gauge on the instrument measured the air pressure in the tank. As tight as the seating was I can only say that the two men in the car would have to be very close friends.

The straight-through exhaust made a mighty sound for such a little engine!

The blower was not designed to run constantly, but was actuated by depressing the accelerator to the floor. The blower ran at 2.2 times engine speed, and gave a sudden surge of power, accompanied by a high whine of the blower gears. When Lord Ridley owned the car, he tested the engine on his brake and found the engine produced 54 horsepower unblown at 4000 rpm and 79 horsepower with the blower engaged, producing 6 psi boost. Maximum rpm was 4500. Unlike the later Alfas, the compressor blew through the carburetor, so when it was not engaged, a valve opened to draw induction air via a tube that crossed over to the other side of the engine where it was heated by the exhaust. Like the engine's beginnings, it was rather tortuous.

Even after advertising the Mercedes extensively, the best offer we had for the car was from Bob Sutherland, who had by then begun his car collection in Denver. Bob was especially interested in racing cars, and he had the help of Mike Dopudja, a very capable mechanic in the Denver area. Mike could continue to sort out the little Mercedes' problems after the engine was completely broken in. In the spring of 1976, Bob paid $38,500 for it, so my half was $19,250. I'm sure it cost more than that to restore, but it was most certainly a worthwhile effort to save a very historic automobile.

In spite of having extremely bad eyesight, Bob Sutherland drove the car at Steve Earle's third annual Historic Races at Laguna Seca in a race for the oldest racing cars. It was then exhibited the following Sunday at the Pebble Beach Concours d'Élégance, August 29, 1976. Bob sold the car a few years later, and I have completely lost track of it. It really was not very practical to drive with much pleasure, so it no doubt has been put on display in some museum, perhaps even the factory museum in Stuttgart.

These three Targa Florio Mercedes are too rare to have an established value. They were historically important because they broke new ground for Mercedes, and their value would be as a museum piece, rather than a practical road car. I would guess it to be worth about $300,000.

10

The 1957
Gullwing Mercedes

My good friend, Gene Rouse, bought a nice low mileage 300SL Gullwing Mercedes, and in 1960 he bought a new 300SL Roadster. I drove both of these cars a bit, and they were simply amazing for their time. Gene didn't drive them much because he didn't want to put a lot of mileage on them. I nagged him to drive them enough to keep the seals lubricated but he kept them under covers in his storage building just up the street from my sign plant. For a family car Gene bought a very good-looking new Mercedes 220SE Coupe in 1965. The coupe, built in the Sindelfingen factory, was more expensive and better looking than the standard four-door sedans, its body lacking the sedan's little tailfins. Gene's was ivory with saddle leather, with a manual transmission and floor-mounted shifter.

Having few stand-alone dealers when they reentered the U.S. market, Mercedes made a deal with Studebaker for their dealers to also sell and service Mercedes-Benz. But that didn't last long because Studebaker was in deep financial trouble, and soon, Mercedes negotiated dealerships in the larger cities. Denver was a large enough market to justify a dealership with Kumpf Motors, which also sold several other pricey foreign cars such as Rolls-Royce and Jaguar at that time. Gene and I used to stop by Kumpf Motors occasionally when we went to Denver for a Water Pick board meeting. We would look at the new imported cars on the showroom floor and pick up literature that they didn't just hand out to everyone. We would drop a hint that we were down from Fort Collins for our board meeting. I was amused by the fake British accent the Jaguar and Rolls-

Royce salesmen put on, as well as their use of "boot" for the trunk, "hood" for the convertible top and "bonnet" for the hood. And of course, the Rolls-Royce came with a full set of "spanners" in a beautiful, fitted toolbox. These salesmen may have worked in theatre at night.

Even though it was now twenty years after Hitler's devastation of Europe, Mercedes was still struggling to recover their prewar reputation for fine engineering. They were also promoting Mercedes as the safest cars in the world, even distributing a film through their dealers that showed their top of the line S-Class sedan going over a cliff, end for end, then rolling several times. A man in the film walked up to the wrecked car and opened all four doors! The sheet metal, front and rear, was designed to crumple, absorbing the impact like an accordion, but the passenger compartment was extremely rigid. The front and rear windshields were designed to pop out on impact, and the steering column was padded and canted to go to the right to prevent impaling the driver. The engine mounts were designed to break away and the engine would go under the car instead of into the passenger compartment. And the rear-view mirror and all of the door and window handles would also break away instead of impaling people.

I was so impressed with that film that I also bought my first Mercedes, from Kumpf Motors, a 1965 220SE four-door sedan demonstrator with 5,000 miles on it. Mine was dark blue with red leather. This was the model that had the minuscule tail fins. The 2.2-liter engines (136 cubic inches) were underpowered for the heavy sedans, and weren't very fast in acceleration, but they would run endlessly and quietly at 6,500 rpm, which was more than adequate for highway speeds. The autobahn in Germany, after all, had no speed limit and was the fastest public highway in the world. I quickly came to appreciate the very high build quality and strength of the S-Class Mercedes and for the most part I have driven them as our family cars ever since.

Gene became interested in the big, beautiful pre-war classic Mercedes about the same time I became interested in Alfa Romeos. While Ron Kerr and I were restoring my 8C Alfa Romeo, Gene bought a 500K Special Sindelfingen Roadster from Bill Parfet in Golden and bought a 1929 SS Mercedes Castagna Cabriolet from Vojta Mashek in Chicago. I drove each of these cars a bit, enough to know that I preferred the smaller cars. Admiring and test-driving Gene's 300SLs influenced my decision to take the 1957 300SL Gullwing on trade towards the group of three cars that I sold to Kirk White in 1969. The term "showroom condition" is the standard claim of used car salesmen, but this Gullwing was truly in showroom condition, with very low mileage.

Beginning in 1952 the factory built several lightweight 300SLR racecars, with very beautiful streamlined bodies. They had a five-speed transmission, mounted on the rear deDion axle, and the same straight eight, fuel injected engines as used in the former Mercedes Grand Prix cars. The racing engines produced 310 horsepower at 7400 rpm. Top speed, depending on the axle ratio, was up to 186 mph. Driving a coupe version of the fabulous Mercedes 300SLR, with top-hinged gullwing doors, Stirling Moss, with journalist Denis Jenkinson riding "shotgun," won the 1955 Italian Mille Miglia (1000 mile) race around Italy against all comers, including the best of the Italian cars and drivers. This was a huge victory for Mercedes because the Italian cars and drivers virtually owned the Mille Miglia. It was priceless advertising for Mercedes and it made the young driver, Stirling Moss, world famous overnight. Because these cars had attracted so much attention and amassed so many racing victories, Maximillian (Max) Hoffman, the North American importer for Mercedes, convinced the factory to build the 300SL Gullwing coupes for his affluent American clientele. He guaranteed to sell a sufficient number of these cars to make it profitable for the factory. And he did!

While similar in looks, the production cars were not much like the all-out racing car that Stirling Moss drove to victory in 1955. Hoffman received the first customer's car in March 1955. A total of 1400 Gullwing 300SLs were produced, of which 1100 came to America. The last one was

The beautiful Gullwing Mercedes I took in trade from Kirk White.

manufactured in 1956. They were priced at $8,500, substantially less than a Ferrari, which cost over $11,000 at that time and were still being built in very small numbers. The production version of the 300SL Gullwing was one of the most beautiful sports cars ever produced. It was also state of the art at that time with Mercedes' typically high build quality. They used the three liter six cylinder, single overhead cam engine from the 300SE sedan but with new, direct fuel injection. The motor was tilted at about 45 degrees, to allow the low hood height. They were very civilized sports cars that were also perfectly happy tooling around town, but their character and sounds changed when driven hard.

For stiffness in the lightweight tubular space-frame, the doorsills were so wide that I would sit down on the sill and swing my legs in as I moved into the seat. The steering wheel could be unlocked with a lever, to remove the wheel for easier entry. The interior was trimmed in very high quality leather and the instrument panel was beautifully laid out with a huge tachometer and speedometer in a pod. The car had a good heater but no air conditioner, and although there were vent windows, the side windows were fixed, so the car was very hot to drive in summer even with the fresh air and fan controls on high.

The engine compartment was highly detailed, but I think my car must have had some extra polishing of the aluminum air intake tubes; the cam cover was also highly finished. With fuel injection the rated horsepower was 215, and depending on the axle ratio one could order from the factory, they did zero to sixty in a little less than ten seconds, with a top speed of 145. As fine as they were, they still were not perfect. They soon gained a reputation for suddenly changing their steering characteristics on a hard, fast curve, due to a high polar moment of the rear swing axle that could cause an unprepared driver to lose control of the car.

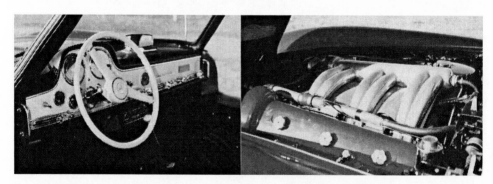

The steering wheel was removable for easy entry. The engine was tilted sideways.

It so happened that I had just finished the restoration of one of the earliest Ferrari GT cars, a 1955 Ferrari 250 GT with a Boano body. We had totally rebuilt the Ferrari and I had been driving it to break the engine in properly and to get it tuned right. The engine displacement was three liters, the same as the Mercedes, but with twelve cylinders. The horsepower was 240 at 7,000 rpm. This particular Ferrari had a rather low axle gear ratio, resulting in a top speed of "only" 135 mph, but a zero to sixty time of about seven seconds.

There was a rather sharp, uphill bend on a road near my home on which I liked to test the steering and handling when I was breaking in a car we had restored. I tried both the 300SL and the 250 GT Ferrari several times on this bend while accelerating hard. I could definitely feel the change in the 300SL's steering, but knowing of its reputation, I was always ready for it. The Gullwing's tail would start to swing in the opposite direction one steered, but a flick of the wheel in the same direction the tail was headed would correct it. The Ferrari, with a fixed rear axle and leaf springs, definitely had the better handling, and it was considerably faster. The Ferraris were still virtually hand built, and therefore were less refined cars at that time. The GT Ferrari was built with a de-tuned racing engine, while the Mercedes had a tuned-up version of a luxury sedan engine in a more refined chassis. Both cars still had big drum brakes. It was interesting for me to be able to compare the two cars of the same vintage. Regardless, I really liked to drive the Mercedes better for pleasure simply because it was so much more refined with a more comfortable ride. And I drove it a lot.

When I finally decided to sell the Gullwing, in spite of continuous advertising, it took over a year to get $9,000 for it from a nice couple from the Oregon coast that came to see it and drive it home. When they bought the car I told them that I sincerely believed they could keep the car as long as they wished and always at least get their money back. They kept it for at least fifteen years that I am aware of. When I told them that I had no idea they would get their money back forty times over!

The Sports Car Market Price Guide *values an equally good 300SL Gullwing Mercedes at $350,000!*

11

The SSK Mercedes

The last car Ron Kerr restored was a genuine 1929 SSK Mercedes. Gene Rouse discovered this car more or less by accident after becoming the marketing director for Teledyne Water Pic. While attending a dental conference in Washington, D.C., he met a local dentist who was also interested in old cars. He told Gene he knew of an old Mercedes roadster in D.C. Gene got the owner's name and made an appointment to see it. The owner had been in the military during World War II. He had seen this old car on a car lot as he commuted back and forth to work, and stopped

The SSK as Gene bought it. Originally there were no bumpers.

The instruments, controls and the entire cockpit were in sad condition.

to look at it. He didn't know what it was, but he bought it for practically nothing. As happens with many well-intentioned people, he intended to fix it up, but never found the time or money. He had owned it ever since, but had not driven it for many years. It was covered and stored in his barn.

Gene was very doubtful that this could be an SSK and was surprised when it was uncovered because it looked correct in spite of the dirt and its sorry condition. Only thirty-three were built, so he knew it was extremely rare, if it was genuine. The man said he would sell it for about $10,000. Gene said he would get back to him the next day. He called Bud Cohn, a well-known Mercedes guru in Los Angeles who owned an SS Mercedes. Bud told him it probably was not a genuine SSK because there were only a few known SSKs in the world. Gene told the man he would check it out when he returned home and get back to him. Sure enough, the numbers checked out. The SSK was genuine! And it was entirely original and all there. The wind-wings and bumpers were not original, and the honeycomb radiator would not hold water.

Of course Gene bought the car, and had it shipped home. He asked if we would restore it for him. We didn't have room for the whole car, but I agreed that Ron could do the basic engine rebuild at our plant. Gene had bought a small showroom and garage down the street from our sign plant

The 1929 SSK Mercedes in the Rouse family room—on the Biltmore golf course.

that had been the dealership for Studebaker in their final death throes. (I had my first drive in an Avanti there.) Gene kept his Gullwing, a Mercedes SS Castagna Cabriolet and his brand new 300SL Roadster there. Ron finished the basic rebuild of the engine at our shop pretty quickly because we needed the space. Because the crankshaft was so long, we had to have the crankshaft ground and the babbitt bearings cast and the align-boring done by a diesel engine company in Denver. These engines were huge, over three times the displacement of my 8C-2.3 Alfa engine, and didn't put out much more power. Starting with Mercedes' big, slow-revving stationary engines Ferdinand Porsche had developed the engines for the long chassis S, the SS and the short chassis SSKs. The power to displacement ratio was not good, thus the big "elephant" blower was needed to get the heavy cars moving quickly. With hindsight, Ron and I both tended to over-restore the engine compartments by doing more polishing and plating than was originally done by the factory. We didn't know any better then. Bud Cohn helped Gene with a source to remake the square-tube, V-shaped radiator core, and sold him a few things from his horde of precious original factory parts.

Ron restored the rest of the car in Gene's building in his spare time, but it took several years to finish the entire car. By the time the SSK was finished Gene was president of Teledyne Water Pic and had built a beautiful big home on the Biltmore golf course in Phoenix. Gene kept the car inside in the family room. Just outside its big windows was the fourth fair-

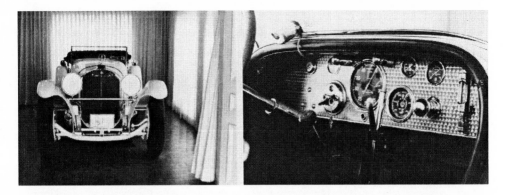

Doors from the garage were hidden by drapes. Ron made the new instrument panel.

way and nearby was one of the Tee-boxes. The drapes were usually left open so golfers could admire the car before they'd tee off. I imagine the Mercedes slowed the play down quite a bit. The large garage was just beyond this room with a connecting door and ramp so the car could be taken into or out of the house at any time. Gene very seldom drove his cars in spite of my nagging him to do so. I tried to convince him that they needed to be driven enough to keep the seals from drying out and leaking.

I was never attracted to the big old Mercedes because they were such huge, heavy, brutal cars compared to the Alfa Romeos and Bugattis of the same period. I had driven Gene's SS Castagna Cabriolet when it was delivered to Fort Collins and it took all my strength to handle it. The steering at low speeds was incredibly heavy, and to stop the car I virtually had to stand on the brake pedal, with very little results I must add, and the clutch and shifting were equally heavy and ponderous. I'm sure an SSK was much better, especially at speed when the steering would be much lighter than driving it around town in traffic. I can't imagine trying to parallel park it. I gained real respect for the great German drivers, such as Lang and especially Caracciola, who made his reputation competing with an SSK. Aware of the notoriously poor brakes, I always gave myself two or three hundred feet of extra stopping distance the few times I drove one of Gene's old brutes. Admittedly, the SSK was a good deal lighter, with a short chassis and aluminum body, but it could not really compare in any respect to an Alfa or Bugatti. I kidded Gene that what Mercedes did with a battle-axe, Alfa Romeo did with a rapier, but you can never fault Gene's ability to spot where the big money is. He was not only smarter than me—he was also a lot luckier!

Unlike me, Gene is a true collector of things. His cars were investments. And unlike me, he was affluent enough to be a collector. Classic
Mercedes became quite valuable long before the Alfa Romeos did, but that
didn't change my preference for Alfa Romeos over Mercedes. Eventually,
the Alfas not only caught up, but certain models, like the 8C-2.9 Roadsters, passed all of them except possibly the SSK. The enormous value of
a genuine SSK is largely because there are only a few survivors. According to recent claims there are only three.

Unlike the Alfa's Roots blower, which was engaged full time, the
"Elephant" blower on the SSK was only used for a burst of speed of short
duration. It is clutch operated by pressing the accelerator hard to the floor
and holding it down until the blower is to be disengaged. It virtually
screamed when engaged, probably scaring the hell out of anyone in front
of the SSK to make the driver jam on the brakes and move over! They may
have thought they were about to get run over by a train. Maybe that's how
the passing was really done by Caracciola when he raced the SSK.

Nevertheless, Gene got even with my cracks about his SSK. They are
among the world's most valuable automobiles and when Gene finally sold
his SSK, in the late eighties I think it was, it was worth a whole lot of
money. The *Sports Car Market Price Guide* values an SSK from $6 to $8
million, one very recently reputedly sold at auction for over $7 million.
And it needed a full restoration! And it didn't even have the original body!
I freely admit that Gene is just smarter than I am when it comes to anything concerning money, but my Alfas were eventually more valuable than
his Mercedes, a moot point now that neither of us owns them.

If Gene had kept his SS Castagna Cabriolet, and had it restored, it
would have a market value of about $700,000 today. Shortly after he bought
the Castagna Cabriolet from Vojta Mashek, he also bought that gorgeous

Two views of the vertical "Elephant" blower.

supercharged 500K Special Roadster from Bill Parfet, but he sold it soon afterwards for a good profit. It had the Sindelfingen body with red paint-work and light tan leather with the big outside chrome plated exhaust pipes.

Those and the 540K Special Roadsters are now the next most valuable Mercedes according to the Sportscar Market Price Guide. *They are each worth about $2,500,000 on today's market. The SSK Roadsters are valued from $6,000,000 to $8,000,000.*

12

The 1953 212
Inter Ferrari #0289 EU

By 1973, not having found another supercharged Alfa Romeo, I found the next best thing: a 1953 Ferrari 212 Inter coupe, with an all aluminum body by Vignale. I bought it for $4,500 from Tom Oleson, who always seemed to have a used Ferrari for sale in those days. The engine was in pieces and it was missing its intake manifold and carburetors. It had been put out of commission by a faulty cylinder liner casting that resulted in a hole in the cylinder wall. We then knew very little of the car's early history, except that some previous owners were J. Florio, Tom Butt and Dick Merritt. History didn't seem to be so important in regard to their relatively small value then.

While this book is not intended to be about the details of restoration work, I will take this one car as an example for those who may want to know what is necessary to restore an early Ferrari or any other similar car. Keep in mind that, except for the V-12 engines, these cars were actually quite simple and straightforward compared to a modern car. The biggest problem for a Ferrari at that time was acquiring parts if they were needed. However, we had learned that almost any part could be rebuilt if new parts were unavailable, or if the cost of new parts was prohibitive.

General Procedure

It is always very helpful to be able to drive a car before dismantling it to determine what may be right and especially to ascertain what is wrong with it. However, our routine practice in restoring any car was to dismantle the engine, the cooling system, the transmission, the rear axle, the whole suspension system, the brake system and all the ancillary equipment such as the wiring, starter, generator, fuel and water pumps, the distributors, the clutch and drive shaft. Since it must be dismantled, I was not necessarily deterred if a car was already apart because we had to take them apart anyway. I was much more concerned that it was all there. In fact, I bought some real basket cases.

Once dismantled, every part should be examined to determine the need to restore it cosmetically, rebuild it or replace it. All critical parts, such as the crankshaft and connecting rods, should be magnafluxed, especially on a high performance engine like the Ferrari. We routinely replace every bearing, bushing and seal on the car. High-strength rod and main bolts should always be replaced if at all possible. I have experienced a couple of engine failures that were caused by rod bolts that had stretched.

The Ferrari engine block, heads, sump, transmission case, brake drums (with shrunk-in steel liners) and the differential carrier are cast aluminum. When dismantled, every part is sandblasted or glass-beaded to return the external surface to its original condition, free of all oil or grease stains, or of any paint. Those aluminum parts that are not to be painted are sealed with a clear finish to prevent future oil and dirt stains penetrating the metal. This should be a clear finish that will not discolor with time and heat. The internal surfaces of the engine and transmission are boiled out in a solution that is compatible with aluminum then painted inside with red glyptal that prevents oil seepage into the pores of the aluminum, aids rapid oil drainage and prevents sludge build-up.

Engine

The metal panels of this Ferrari's engine compartment were pretty crude, as could be seen by the louvers and the cut made for the battery shelf so the battery could project partly into the wheel-well. The engine still had the inside plugs and the front-mounted distributors.

To remove the shrunk-in liners we heated the block to 140 degrees in our oven to press out the steel cylinder liners. We sandblasted the outside of the liners and the inside the block to remove all the scale so they would transfer heat from the cylinders to cool the engine as when it was new. We bought one new liner and machined it to match the others, which showed virtually no wear. We honed all the liners and had new Jahns pistons made to match the original Borgo pistons. The Jahns pistons came with rings

The 212 Inter engine with three Weber carburetors and air cleaner.

and wrist pins. I understand that Jahns is no longer in business, but there are several other manufacturers if new factory pistons are not available. The pistons should be weighed and balanced with a good scale, such as a postage scale. Beginning with the lightest piston, weight can be removed from the skirts of the others until they all match.

The early Ferrari crankshafts were nitrided to harden the surface. If the crankshaft is to be turned undersize, the nitride surface is destroyed and should be re-hardened after grinding. If the shaft merely needs polishing that will not damage the nitride surface. Diesel engine machinists are a good source for critical crankshaft work. The crankshaft should also be balanced. The 212's shaft was ground .010", the first undersize, and fitted with new Vandervell main and rod bearings. Thrust is taken by the end main bearings, which must provide a slight endplay.

The original valves were not worn, but had they been, valves can be rebuilt by hard-facing and hard chroming the stems, then grinding them to original size and hand-lapping the faces and seats. All valve springs and the bronze guides were good. If the bronze guides are only slightly worn they can be knurled for a closer tolerance, but they should have about .002" clearance. The camshafts were in very good condition and required no repairs. Camshaft specialists can straighten and regrind them to the original profile if necessary. The heads were checked for flatness and were only skimmed to clean up the surfaces.

We routinely replace timing chains, rebuild the water pumps with new diaphragms, bearings and seals, resurface the flywheel and rebuild the clutch. All roller and ball bearings are metric sizes, so there is no difference between foreign and American made bearings. All that is needed for replacement is the bearing make and number stamped into the bearing race, or just the outer and inner diameters and the width. If a bearing has frozen and turned in the housing, the housing can be machined for a sleeve that can be chilled and pressed in place. When the engine is reassembled, it should be statically and dynamically balanced for smooth running. Aircraft engine machine shops are a good source for this sort of balancing.

Clutch and Transmission

This five-speed and reverse transmission had synchromesh on third, fourth and fifth gears only. The gears were in excellent condition. The clutch release fork was worn, so we had it hard-faced and machined. The clutch springs were tested and were good, so they were set at 31 mm as specified for this model. The non-synchronized first and second gears take some getting used to, but the transmission was smooth and quiet in our bench test, using an electric motor with reduction gear. The two-piece drive shaft bearings were bad and were replaced. The universal joints were good. Any two-piece drive shaft should be marked to reassemble it the same way it came apart. Balancing the drive shaft is very important.

Rear Axle

This 212 Inter axle had an 8 × 40 (5:0 to 1) ratio, which was good for acceleration or hill climbing but limited the top speed to about 135 mph. We found badly worn ring and pinion gears in the differential. There are seven bearings in the axle assembly, including the outer shaft bearings. Thrust is taken by a large double-row bearing. There is no pre-load on this type of differential. Machined spacers separate the bearings and they must be precise. It was necessary to machine a sleeve for the carrier housing as it had been damaged by improper assembly at some time which allowed the front pinion bearing to turn in its housing. All bearings were replaced and new spacers were machined to set the backlash at .004". In spite of all this, the rear axle proved to be noisy due to the worn ring and pinion gears, so I ordered a new ring and pinion from David Clarke in England. We were also advised by Fred Leydorf, who was then the technical advisor for the Ferrari Club of America, to set the backlash even closer, on the order of .0015" to .002". Fred was a great help to Ferrari owners in those days.

Brakes

Having been stored for about ten years, the brake fluid had gelled and ruined the lines and hoses. The entire brake system had to be rebuilt with new master and wheel cylinder parts. The original metric kit parts were no longer available so we honed the cylinders to accept U.S. repair kits. New brake hoses and lines were installed. The finned aluminum drums with shrunk-in cast iron (or steel) liners were sandblasted and the drums were turned. New brake linings were installed and arched. New drum brakes take some time to bed the linings to fit perfectly. I always drove the cars and braked hard for quite a while, then removed the wheels to inspect the linings to see the wear pattern.

Shock Absorbers

The 212 Inter has four single lever-type hydraulic double-acting Houdaille shock absorbers. No one was offering Houdaille service at that time, and we were not equipped to dismantle them. We filled them with carburetor cleaner and soaked them until they worked freely then flushed them out, filled them with castor oil, and adjusted them in a vise to equal amount of resistance. There are now advertisements for service facilities for Houdaille shocks.

Suspension System

The kingpins, bushings and steering linkage were all in good condition. These are critical to a car's handling, steering and safety and must always be replaced or rebuilt if there is any play. We adjusted the steering gear play by turning the eccentric collar as required and installed new bearings and oil seal.

Body and Paint Work

The old paint finish was stripped to the bare aluminum. Using a proper primer for aluminum is critical. The best paint we had at that time was Imron, a vast improvement over enamel or lacquer for durability but difficult to repair. We elected to refinish this car with dark red lacquer that was close to Ferrari's racing color, with a final clear coat to be buffed. The end result was a near show quality finish. I was never interested in showing the car, but we wanted the car to look as good as we could make it look within a reasonable cost.

Wheels and Tires

The original wheels are 15" Borranis with alloy rims and steel spokes. Originally they were not polished and plated, but painted. We fitted new 165 × 15 ZX Michelin radial tires. Driving and handling can be greatly improved by putting radial tires on any car that was originally fitted with bias-ply tires.

One of the most delightful things about these very early Ferraris that were built in such small numbers are the many clues that show the bodies and trim pieces were being virtually hand made. That was especially true on this 212 Inter. Many of the small hardware pieces and fittings were unique, made especially for just this car, or perhaps for a few others like it. One small example was the egg-crate grill that is convex in two directions. It was in bad shape, and to make a new one, including the beveled oval polished aluminum surround, took Loran three weeks.

The rake of the seat back was adjusted by a knurled thumbscrew to a fixed position. The doorsills have a hand-made aluminum cover that is engraved with wavy lines that match the engraving on the hand-made steering wheel spokes. Even the rear view mirror is unique. It has a vertical rod to allow the mirror to be moved several inches up or down, or to swivel sideways, then be locked into place with a clamp to prevent vibration. Even the opaque Plexiglas sun visors are beautiful. The leather trimmed dash panel has a polished aluminum half-round trim piece that meets the same trim near the top of the doors. The carpeted side-panels have a fresh air vent that can be opened to cool the feet and legs. A carpeted bench behind the seats is large enough for a small suitcase, with straps to hold it down.

Note that this car is left-hand drive, possibly for export to the original owner. Loran and I thought the car had been used in competition such

The restored leather interior. Note the left-hand steering.

as hill-climbs, road rallies, or even circuit racing. The trunk space is almost entirely taken up by a huge gas tank with the spare tire strapped on top. The flip-top filler cap is so large that I would reach down into the tank with a Coke bottle if I needed a little gasoline for something. Also, the wear in the rear axle indicated a lot of hard use. There was a Tachomedian instrument in the center of the dash, normally only installed on competition cars. It told the average speed of a trip, until it was reset. It had a small clock inset in the Tachomedian with a sweep-second hand with another regular clock in the instrument cluster. An instrument like this would only be useful in a rally. Also, the all aluminum body with Plexiglas windshields reduced the weight substantially.

The outside door handles are recessed into the doors in a flush polished aluminum housing. A button is pushed which brings the handle out of its housing, then the door is opened by pulling the handle farther out. The front door jambs are faced with hand-fitted brass panels that are

Restored Ferrari 212 Inter no. 0289EU with Vignale body.

chrome plated. The rear jamb faces are aluminum, painted to match the body.

I was able to find the proper intake manifold and three two-choke carburetors in England. I got the proper jetting information for the carburetors from Steven Griswold, who had tested his 212 Inter coupe that produced 170 horsepower on a dynamometer. I drove this car for quite a while. It was very pleasant and comfortable to drive, with a lot of acceleration. After breaking the engine in and fine-tuning it a bit I sold the car to Fred Jaeger of Racine, Wisconsin, in 1976, for $17,500. I know that Fred kept the car for many years. I have seen it advertised once or twice over the years, but I don't know where it is today.

It is hard to believe that there was very little interest in such cars at that time. People were buying new Ferraris in ever-greater numbers, but only a few people, like myself, cared enough to restore the old ones. Loran had about 1200 hours in this project, in addition to the outside costs for machine work, parts and upholstery. I lost about $4,000, for the privilege of saving another historic car. But for me, it was a work of love. If its early history is known now, and if it was raced, with its aluminum body it would probably be worth about $750,000 at the present time.

The Sports Car Market Price Guide *values an ordinary 212 Inter at $800,000.*

13

The Talbot Lagos

I first became interested in Talbot Lagos (pronounced tal-bo-lah-go) through John O'Donnell, who had brought several to the U.S. through Bart Loyens, the broker in Luxembourg. I had subscribed to *Automobile Quarterly* since it began publication in 1962 and I had a growing library of automobile books. Every photo I saw of a Talbot Lago credited Mr. Vojta Mashek, Jr., of Chicago as the owner. I had corresponded with Vojta (pronounced Voita) about his 8C-2.3 Alfa Romeo Cabriolet. When I had a business trip to Chicago, I arranged for Gene Rouse and me to see Vojta's automobile collection, which he kept in several buildings on his country estate in southwestern Michigan. He and his wife were most gracious to us. As a retired Chicago mortgage broker, he was obviously well off. Raised in an affluent neighborhood, he developed his taste for fine European automobiles because he saw and admired them driving around Chicago when they were new. He began buying them at used car prices when they were worth very little.

With over fifty cars, all in beautiful, restored condition, it was the most fabulous private collection of the most desirable cars I have ever seen. Recalling my first car book, *Cars of the Connoisseurs*, I could see that Vojta not only had every make described in that book, he also had the most desirable models, the best years of manufacture and the best body styles as well. His collection reflected an impeccable taste in cars. He also had many makes that Mr. Buckley's limited book did not include. And that's where I first saw a Talbot Lago in the flesh—three of them, in fact. Two had beautiful French coachwork and the third was a competition car with a Dutch-built body. I was determined to find and buy a Talbot Lago to restore.

The Saoutchik Talbot Lago as it was when I bought it.

With the metal top removed. I was afraid it was too far gone to save.

I soon discovered they were even scarcer than 8C Alfa Romeos. After I had watched the car magazine ads for months, Marvin Newman of Columbus, Ohio, advertised a derelict 1948 Talbot Lago Gran Sport with a body by Saoutchik of Paris. His letter and Polaroid pictures indicated that it was indeed in very bad condition, with all the wood rotted out, but that the car was all there and original. I bought it for $2,400 in December 1973. In spite of Mr. Newman's description, when Ron began to dismantle it, it was much worse than I expected, so bad that I was afraid we would have to junk it. My imagination always tends to paint pretty pictures. We came to the conclusion that this car had been in a flood or damaged by water at some time.

Of the French designers of that period Saoutchik was one of the most flamboyant. After Ron dismantled the car I carefully sandblasted the body and discovered that the steel body panels were hand-formed in relatively small sections, with overlapping joints, *nailed* to a hardwood frame! And the nails had almost rusted away. This crude method of construction surprised me, until it occurred to me that the war had probably taken all the metal and that this body may have been made from remnants of metal. The body was then covered with a coat of very hard putty of some sort and sanded smooth to cover all these joints, then painted.

Loran Swanson took over when Ron left. They had to make the entire white ash wood framework new. Very little of the original wood was usable, even for patterns. Instead of using common nails to refasten the metal to the wood frame, Loran used copper nails that would never rust. I had some experience with making fiberglass figures for advertising displays shortly after that material was introduced. I suggested that he should also bond the backside of the metal panels to the wood frame with glass fiber and polyester resin. That made the wood frame and metal skin into a very rigid struc-

The wood was completely rotten—some completely gone!

The restored Type 26 Gran Sport Talbot Lago chassis no. 110114.

ture, much stronger than the original. This car turned out to be one of the biggest challenges we ever met. First Ron, then Loran worked on it intermittently for five years! We never hesitated to use modern materials, like the fiberglass, to improve the body structure, where it would not be seen.

Antonio Lago had taken over the moribund French division of Sunbeam-Talbot-Darracq. Being Italian, he went racing to sell his cars. His 4.5 liter unblown Grand Prix cars had considerable success because of their reliability and because they required fewer pit stops for fuel than their more powerful, but thirstier, 1.5 liter supercharged competitors. The engine of the 104-inch wheelbase Grand Sport Talbot Lago was based on a robust, seven main bearing six-cylinder block. Unable to afford a totally new engine, Lago designed a new head with hemispherical combustion chambers with a unique rocker system that worked the overhead valves by short push rods from twin camshafts mounted high in the block. It gave the appearance of a double overhead cam engine. The early Grand Sport engines had three carburetors and produced 190 horsepower.

There were virtually no English language manuals for Talbot Lagos, and very little literature in French. Through John O'Donnell and a few owners, we gathered enough basic technical information, such as for the valve and ignition timing, to rebuild the engine. They were equipped with a four-speed Wilson pre-selector gearbox that was used in both racing and sports cars. These Wilson gearboxes were widely used in England, where they were manufactured, so I found a manual for adjusting the transmission. These were very strong transmissions, and this one had not been damaged. The Wilson pre-selector transmission was pleasant to use, somewhat like the Cord, but all mechanical. You would put the column shift in the gear position you wished, and nothing happened until you jabbed the foot pedal (there was no clutch); then it shifted *immediately*! The Talbot Lagos were right-hand drive cars with very wide, spacious seats for the

The Talbot Lago Saoutchik in Clive Cussler's collection.

period. However, the headroom in the Saoutchik body was insufficient for me, making the car uncomfortable to drive very far. These bodies were built for looks, not comfort. Following our usual methods of totally dismantling every nut and bolt, we were finally able to return the car to its original elegance.

In 1978 I sold the Talbot Lago to Clive Cussler, the author, for $32,500, equal to about $100,000 in 2005 dollars, and worth five or six times as much now. My wife and I took Clive and his wife to lunch at the Fort Collins Country Club. They are both charming, interesting people. Even then Clive was talking about hunting for sunken treasure ships. They lived in Golden at that time. I asked if he lived in the mountains, with a grand view to draw upon for inspiration. He said no, that he wrote in his basement, with a blank wall facing him. I believe he told me that at one time he wrote advertising copy for a living. He had just sold the movie rights to his book, *Raise the Titanic.* If not the first, this purchase of my Talbot Lago was near the first of his car collection. He called to tell me that he had a flat driving the car home, due to a pinched inner tube! When

I last saw him, the car was still in his collection, near Golden, Colorado. Jackie recently read Cussler's 1984 book *Deep Six* in which Clive features this Talbot Lago. He included a drawing of it. Unfortunately it was blown up in the story, but Dirk Pitt wasn't in it!

Because the Saoutchik Talbot Lago was going to take so long to finish, I still wanted a nice, running car. I bought a beautiful short wheelbase Talbot Lago cabriolet, with one-off body by DuBos, from Anthony Bamford in England. He had bought the car from someone on the island of Majorca. I had it shipped to the Port of New York where John O'Donnell was good enough to pick it up and ship it on to me. Ocean freight was surprisingly inexpensive. It was truly a beautiful car, and in excellent running condition. Finally, I could drive a Talbot Lago to experience firsthand what they were like. Except for one thing: I could hardly drive it because the beautiful big steering wheel was right in my chest and there was no seat adjustment. With little room for my long legs, operating the brake and "clutch" pedal was very awkward. A really tall man would not have been able to drive it at all. It was a very fast sports car with good handling for its time, but that spoiled it for me. I decided to keep it long enough to learn what we might need to know to finish the Saoutchik, then sell the DuBos to get something else.

They were good for about 125 mph, with huge, finned hydraulic brakes. One could tell the fine Italian hand of Tony Lago in the chassis design and by how well the car handled. They were definitely a fine sports car.

I disproved a rumor that this had been Prince Rainier's car by writing the Palace in Monaco. His secretary wrote back that the Prince had owned Talbot Lagos, and while mine was beautiful, unfortunately, it had never been the Prince's car. The only thing Loran did to this car was to repaint it and install new tires. The original blue finish was still pretty fair, but would no longer take a shine. I selected a very nice Mercedes color that had a slight violet cast.

I had become well acquainted with Peter Giddings, who was seriously into vintage racing and had one of the Talbot Lago Grand Prix singleseater racecars. That car, however, was one of the early, less powerful racers and he was trying to buy one of the later, more powerful 4.5-liter Grand Prix cars from Lindley Locke, in California. Peter showed Mr. Locke pictures of my DuBos bodied car, and he liked it so much he was willing to sell Peter the Grand Prix car if he could buy my DuBos. So to help Peter get his Grand Prix Talbot Lago, I agreed to sell it, even though I was not really ready to do so. Lindley and his wife Betty came to see the car and were guests in our home. A three-cornered deal was struck whereby Peter

The 1949 short wheelbase Type 26 Talbot Lago with DuBos body.

The cockpit was tight. Note the column-mounted Wilson Pre-selector gear lever.

got his Grand Prix car, the Lockes got the DuBos Talbot Lago and I just got some money. I don't even remember how much, but nothing like what it's worth today. The short wheelbase DuBos Talbot Lago Grand Sport would probably be worth about a half million dollars. As a rule of thumb, any convertible car is worth more than a closed version of the same car, and most Talbot Lagos were coupes. This particular Talbot Lago was the sole subject of a feature article in the April 1987 issue of *Motor Trend*, written by John Ethridge with photography by David Gooley.

I corresponded with A.S. Carroll of Pennsylvania, one of the few American owners of Talbot Lagos. He owned two and wanted to sell his 1954, one of the last Talbot Lago GSLs (the L was for long chassis). It had the same 4.5-liter, three-carburetor engine as used in the Grand Prix cars, except detuned for street use. Nevertheless these last engines were rated at 210 horsepower. Because both of my previous Talbot Lagos had short wheelbases and were uncomfortable for me to drive, I bought the GSL, paying very little because it had a cracked block. When we got the car and dismantled it, we sent the whole engine to Precision Babbitt and Engine Works in Hastings, Nebraska, who did the engine machine work, including casting and machining two new cylinder sleeves to repair the cracked block. We did a complete restoration of the car.

This was a factory body—not as flamboyant as the custom bodies, but a very good looking automobile. The interior featured very wide seats and a beautiful steering wheel with the pre-selector shift quadrant on the right and the light-flasher and air-horn levers on left of the wheel.

The above cars are featured in *Automobile Quarterly*, Volume 23, No. 4. Because the GSL was a long wheelbase car, it proved to be much more comfortable to drive, with plenty of legroom. It was everything a very good sports coupe should have been in the mid–1950s. The top speed was less than that of a Ferrari road car, but more practical for normal driving. The body was a custom design, of very good construction, but was factory built. I drove this car quite a bit to break in the engine and to tune it before it was sold. For anyone wanting to buy a Talbot Lago to drive, I recommend the long-chassis cars, unless the driver is not over 5'8" tall, and only weighs about 150 pounds.

I especially liked the design of the derrière of these French cars. It may have been the very beginning of the wedge-shape that later dominated car styling. The huge polished aluminum brake drums that totally filled the beautiful chrome wire wheels were not only pretty—they stopped the car!

In the early days of automobiles France had been in the forefront of the infant industry and was the first country to sponsor racing. Until World War II some of the world's finest, fastest and most beautiful automobiles were built in France. But after the war the socialist French government imposed such high taxes on luxury automobiles that it brought an end to those companies that manufactured them. Tony Lago was among the last to build such cars. By 1955 his production had dwindled to a trickle. In an attempt to hang on he designed a smaller, less expensive coupe aimed at the growing American sports car market. At first, it had a 2.5 liter four cylinder engine, and in its very last gasp, it was called the Lago America, with a BMW 2.5-liter V-8 engine. But these cars proved to be too expen-

1954 4.5-liter Type 26 Gran Sport GSL (long wheelbase chassis).

A very wide, roomy cockpit. Note the beautiful big steering wheel.

sive to compete in the U.S. market that was now flooded with inexpensive British sports cars.

Without learning to read French, I had learned about everything I could about Talbot Lagos, and after selling this car in 1978, I was ready to relegate Talbot Lagos to my growing list of fond memories. And I did—until I happened to see an ad right here in Colorado for a 1955 Talbot Lago 2500, one of those last-gasp efforts of Tony Lago's to keep his company afloat. By this time, the smaller cars had an excellent Z-F four-speed floor-

The detuned Gran Prix engine produced 210 hp with three side-draft Webers.

The 1955 four-cylinder Talbot Lago 2500 with factory body.

shift transmission. They looked like a three-quarter-scale version of the big GSL Talbot Lago. These 2.5-liter engines had a bad reputation, but even though I knew I could never recover my cost, I had Loran do a complete restoration, including a new bare-metal paint job, new interior and an engine and transmission rebuild.

Plush, roomy interior. Aluminum doors, hood and trunk lid.

The body was steel, with aluminum doors, hood and trunk lid. To give extra knee room, there was no inner door lining. The front and rear windshields, as well as the sliding side windows, were Plexiglas to save weight, and possibly to save the expense of glass molds for such a small number of cars built.

This car still had that very wide stance, and was quite comfortable for me to drive. They had cost about $4,500 in U.S. dollars when new, and compared to the bigger, more powerful Talbot Lagos, they were a disappointment. They lacked power. I thought that if I ever ran across one of the very last cars, a Lago America, with the BMW engine, I would buy it—but I never did, until many years later, after I had given up my automobile hobby entirely. Besides, they wanted almost $100,000 for it by then. And it needed work!

The four Talbot Lagos I owned would have a current market value of about $1,700,000.

14

The Type 57 Bugatti

"Provenance" is a word that the big-time, international auction firms have chosen to imply authenticity, originality, and known history of ownership without being too specific. For the kind of cars I deal with in this book, the car's racing history has become very important. One might compare this to having a pedigreed dog rather than a mongrel. The mongrel might be just as good, or even a better dog for a pet, but it has little monetary value.

Ettore Bugatti's motto for his factory and his entire enclave was *Pur Sang*, pure blood. His cars, like his stable of fine horses, and his factory were meant to be the very best, all expressions of his own great talent and passion for perfection. He was even very selective about to whom he would sell a car. He maintained a small hotel at Molsheim where a prospective buyer would sometimes be a guest, invited to dine with the Bugatti family. If one's table manners and conversation did not meet Bugatti's expectations, interminable delays culminated in regrets that the automobile the client was so anxious to buy was unavailable!

Most of the cars about which I have written began life as thoroughbreds. Most of them remained that way, and are worth an incredible amount of money today, long after I sold them. But I was never fortunate enough or rich enough to own a *pur sang* 8C 2.3 Alfa Romeo. The only two I found that the owner would sell and I could spare the money to buy were both mongrels. But I loved them dearly, proven by our loving restoration of them.

Some of these types of cars have, in fact, become so valuable that total fakes have been built. But more often, copies of cars like the 8C-2.6 Monza

Alfa Romeo are not genuine, even though they are correct in every respect concerning their looks and the parts comprising them. The factory built only ten Alfa Monzas. Then Scuderia Ferrari modified a few more from 2.3 or 2.6-liter short-chassis cars. All of them were built for winning the world's most significant races, which they did. Because so many people want a Monza but cannot have one, they take the parts from a less valuable 8C Alfa and make a copy. Or, as I finally did, they take a genuine 8C-2.3 liter chassis and build a replica body for it. These cars are no longer *pur sang*—they are mongrels. They are just as beautiful, and they may run and drive just as well, but they are not nearly as valuable. I have been privileged to own and drive six of the great, supercharged Alfas. Only two were pure bred, but the four mongrels were just as good in every respect except value. And I was not in it for money. I was always in it as a hobby. And by the time I sold my last 8C-2.3 Alfa and the 6C-1750 Zagato, the sort of cars I had always been interested in had become so valuable that it was hardly a hobby anymore. It was becoming another business, and I didn't want that. So I quit—for a while.

When I first met John O'Donnell in 1963 at his home in Westfield, New Jersey, he took me to a see a neighbor's Type 35 Gran Prix Bugatti. Now, in those days an Alfa Romeo owner was considered to be very fortunate if a Bugatti owner would condescend to talk to him on somewhat equal terms. Bugattis were the Holy Grail, and were even more valuable than the supercharged Alfas at that time. Built upon countless racing successes the Bugatti legend was nurtured into a cult, primarily by the British enthusiasts. The Bugatti pedigree was even longer than Alfa Romeo's. Admittedly, they were exquisite cars, with wonderfully detailed finish, but they were, in my view, too idiosyncratic. They were the product of one man's genius, an artistic Italian who migrated to France where he was offered the opportunity to design cars when the automobile industry was very young.

I was not particularly interested in having a Bugatti, but when I was visiting John O'Donnell in 1971, he needed some money and I needed another project, so I bought his 1937 Type 57 Bugatti with a Graber cabriolet body. By this time I had read Hugh Conway's definitive book, *Bugatti*, and was thoroughly informed as to their merits and shortcomings. The Type 57 was actually designed by Ettore's son, Jean Bugatti, still using most of the mechanical features his father had designed, but changed enough to be a more practical and straightforward car than those his father designed. I was amused as John took me to see this Bugatti spread over several locations, first to his basement then to three garages he rented around his neighborhood to keep his parts in. I have said that he liked to dismantle cars, but this Bugatti was incredibly dismantled. We spent half a day looking into boxes, crates, fruit jars, and sacks. The only thing that was in one piece was the body, and it would have been dismantled too had it not been in one piece! But I must say that everything was meticulously labeled and I later found that not a single part, not even the smallest screw, was missing when we later assembled the car as we restored it.

Ettore Bugatti built his factory and the family compound in Molsheim, in the Alsatian province of France. It grew into a veritable fiefdom where he ruled over his skilled workers like the martinet aristocrat that he was. Bugatti built production models to support his racing habit, just as Ferrari would do in later years. Ettore was living in Paris while Jean Bugatti managed the factory where he designed the Type 57. The engine consisted of a cast iron cylinder block, mounted to a cast aluminum crankcase with machined aluminum overhead camshaft boxes. The twin camshafts were driven from the rear of the engine with a separate cast aluminum housing. Bugattis were as much an expression of art as they were automobiles, but they also ran—fast!

At the time I bought the Bugatti, Arlen Goodwine, a multi-talented artist, was working for my company as a designer. Arlen never talked much about his parents, but his American father married an English lady and Arlen spent much of his youth in England where he had studied art at

The very highly detailed Type 57 Bugatti engine.

Cambridge. He was a tall, handsome man, the epitome of an English gentleman. He loved cars as much as I did, and enjoyed them vicariously, overseeing the progress in the car shop for me when I was away. I was traveling a lot while the Bugatti was being restored, so Arlen had a lot to do with supervising its restoration. In fact, it was he who said, "Give an Englishman a piece of metal and he will do something silly with it." To prove his point, he made a pair of handsome polished aluminum stone guards for the rear fenders that were the finishing touch the car needed. Arlen also had a wonderful sense of humor. When I admired the compound curved stone guards, he said he had come from a long line of English armor-makers. Arlen also led our company into its first computer software experience by teaching himself to program a Hewlett Packard programmable calculator. This was in the mid–1970s, long before personal computers came along. For Christmas 1977, he gave me an original painting of a "chain-gang" Frazer Nash, so named because they used a set of sprockets and chains instead of a transmission. One can see his fine art training in this piece. He had a great mind and was the best artist that I ever had the pleasure of working with.

Among the most expensive cars in Europe, Bugattis were exquisitely finished with much hand scraping of the cam boxes, engine-turned firewall panels and a great deal of polishing and plating of parts just for their aesthetic value. Bugatti loved to "lace" his components together with a myriad of 8mm bolts. Finished, they were "eye candy" in today's jargon. This was right up Loran's and my alley. We both liked lots of shiny stuff.

Bugatti specified castor oil for his racing cars that were usually stripped and rebuilt after every race. Perhaps the customer was never told to use regular oil in the road cars. I found the reason this particular Bugatti engine failed and had come to its end showing very little use. It had been using castor oil and it had been allowed to sit a long time without being driven or draining the oil. The castor oil had congealed then solidified in the crankshaft and other oil passages, thereby stopping the flow of oil to the bearings. The plugs in the crankshaft webs actually had to be removed in order to drill the rock-hard castor oil out. The same was true in the camshaft oil galleries.

At that time Bunny Phillips was the Bugatti guru. He had been the Bugatti dealer for the West Coast before the war had closed the Bugatti factory. Now getting along in years, he still had a Bugatti restoration shop behind his home in the Los Angeles area. I called him to ask if he would allow Loran Swanson to come and work with him for a couple of weeks to better learn how to rebuild this Type 57 engine. The rest of the car would be no problem. He agreed, and Loran learned a lot of Bunny's

Arlen Goodwine's painting of a "Chain-gang" Frazer Nash.

secrets. Bunny charged us half his regular hourly rate for all the hours Loran worked for him in spite of the fact that Loran did a lot of productive work. Perhaps the most valuable thing Loran learned was how to prevent a Bugatti from leaking oil like a sieve. They were notorious leakers of oil because of all the flat machined mating joints and the mating of dissimilar metals, like aluminum to steel, each with a different rate of expansion. The secret was that Bunny literally glued those parts together with Goodyear Pliobond, a special rubber cement. This sealed the joints, but it also allowed movement between the parts without breaking the seal. The only other thing Loren learned was the very complex method of adjusting the valve clearances, the most complex method I ever heard of.

Loran Swanson was a very talented craftsman who learned best by seeing anything done, but he did not learn things well from a book. In spite of Bunny's teaching, he never quite mastered the valve adjusting methods. This is done for each of the sixteen valves by taking a measurement from the machined surface of the head to the top of the valve stem with a micrometer, measuring and adding the thickness of the hardened cups, then adding the desired clearance, all in centimeters of course. Admittedly, it was very easy to make a mistake. Compared to the Bugatti the Alfa's valve adjustment was simple, fast and easy.

This was the first car we had restored that was very highly finished by the factory. I could begin to see why Bugattisti were so snooty towards us Alfa Romeo guys. But after all, this was a fast, luxurious road car and the Alfas and early Ferraris were built primarily for racing. The Bugatti had hollow, polished front axles and all the tie rod linkage was chrome-plated. The steering gear box was polished aluminum, and the column was chrome-plated steel. It had hydraulic brakes. However, much of the pol-

Note polished aluminum, and chrome plating. Front axles were polished steel.

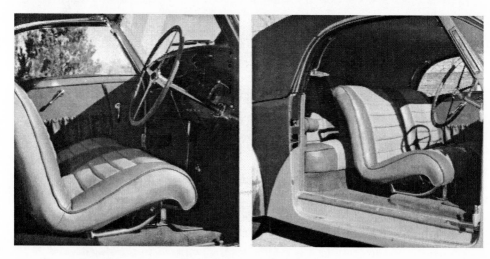

Pumpkin and bronze leather interior with brown convertible top.

The restored Type 57 Bugatti with Graber (of Switzerland) Cabriolet body.

ished steel, such as the axle, and the thousands of small steel bolts were not protected from rust. To preserve the polished and un-plated parts, we clear-coated the polished axle and we cadmium plated the small hardware. We enameled the frame and brake backer-plates with black Imron that, with the chrome, made a beautiful contrast.

As the chassis was being completed, I planned the color scheme for the car by choosing the leather first. Bugatti color combinations were less conservative than most cars. I chose a pumpkin color for the pleated inserts and a complementary warm brown for the rest. The headliner for the padded convertible top was light tan; carpets and cloth top were all coordinated accordingly. I had the paint for the body mixed to match the upholstery, with the darker metallic brown color on top.

Artistic expression was evident everywhere in this car. The springy steel steering wheel with the beautiful wood rim was almost delicate, but strong. Even without formal engineering education, it was said that Ettore Bugatti's engineering instincts were so good that he knew just how lightweight something could be made yet still be adequately strong for the task. He came from a family of artists. He simply chose metal as his métier.

I sold this car in 1974 to a gentleman in New Jersey for $45,000. He insisted on paying for it in cash. Through John O'Donnell I had met Gary Schoenwald, a young attorney who was beginning to collect Alfas and Ferraris. He agreed to meet the buyer in New Jersey and handle the cash through his escrow account. Gary said that when he met the buyer, at night, in New Jersey, he found himself looking over his shoulder. In those

The traditional horseshoe radiator grill.

days, New Jersey was the home of much of the Mafia, and Gary didn't like handling that much cash. That was a lot of money then, equal to $175,000 in today's funny money. I gave the buyer a six month warranty against faulty workmanship or mechanical failure, and sure enough, the buyer found the car was only running on seven cylinders. To keep my word I sent my truck all the way to New Jersey to pick up the car and bring it back to Colorado to find and fix the problem. Loran had made a mistake setting the clearance on one valve and it was not seating properly. Before sending it back, I drove the car about 250 miles, primarily up and down the Poudre River Canyon, to break in the engine, and to be absolutely certain there was nothing more wrong with the car.

The Poudre River Canyon highway is a good road that follows the river for 90 miles. It climbs from 5000 feet in the valley to over 9000 feet to the little town of Walden. There is little traffic in the winter and driving in the canyon was a great and scenic way to break the engine in and seat the rings properly. One is constantly accelerating and decelerating on the curves. It was a lovely and comfortable car to drive, even in winter without a heater in Colorado's mountains. I had made a respectable profit on the car, but this mistake took a big bite out of that profit. I absorbed all that expense just to fix a valve because Loran's arithmetic was not too good. Loran felt so bad he offered to deduct the cost of his mistake from his salary, but he did an otherwise beautiful job on the car, so I just wrote it off to experience. Several times, when I made a good profit on a car that Loran had restored, I would give him a bonus—once it was several thousand dollars.

The buyer was delighted with the car thereafter. He took it to the national meeting of the Antique Automobile Club of America (AACA) in Hershey, Pennsylvania, the largest show in the U.S., where it won First Junior and the following year First Senior Foreign Classic. It also took first place at the national Bugatti Club meet. It was featured in several magazine articles and in *Automobile Quarterly* Volume 21 No. 3.

Bob Sutherland was a Bugatti enthusiast too. He purchased a Type 57 Drophead Coupe that had reputedly belonged to Hugh Conway at one time. Because we were doing my Bugatti, he asked if we would do his chassis at the same time we were doing mine. That made sense. He would have the body done elsewhere. We found that it was literally worn out and when we told Bob his entire chassis was so badly worn that nothing short of a complete restoration could make it right, Bob decided to just have us do the engine and sell the car. We rebuilt his engine simultaneously with ours, but I double-checked Loran's arithmetic when he set the valves on Bob's engine.

Rene Dreyfus was one of France's greatest Gran Prix race-driver of the Bugatti era. While under contract to Bugatti, he came to know Jean Bugatti well. He recalled that Jean was a good, fast driver but that he was reckless. Jean Bugatti was killed while test-driving a Type 57 on a country lane. He swerved to avoid a horse-drawn wagon that came out of a lane. Ettore lost his enthusiasm when he was forced to work under the Nazi occupation, and the company never recovered after the war.

The name has recently been resurrected for a fabulous million-dollar automobile with more than 1,000 horsepower and 250 mph capability, but to me, the car is so far beyond what the original Bugattis were it is unrecognizable as a Bugatti. The current Bugatti super-car is reminiscent of the seven huge Bugatti Royales that Ettore built, extravagant vehicles intended for kings and heads of state. I recall that only three were ever sold. Just as for the Bugatti Royale, it would take a king's ransom to buy one of the new models.

The Type 57 Bugatti was among the last of the beautiful, high-quality automobiles built in France prior to World War II when skill and quality were sufficiently appreciated and there were enough wealthy people to maintain a market for such automobiles.

There is no Sports Car Market Price Guide *value given for a Type 57 Cabriolet, but I would guess at least $450,000.*

15

The 1949 Type 166 Ferrari Barchetta

Enzo Ferrari's passion for racing was extraordinary even for an Italian. He was a successful racing driver for Alfa Romeo in the 1920s but quit driving when his son, Dino, was born in 1931. Ferrari then turned his passion to managing the Alfa Romeo racing team. He organized Scuderia Ferrari where he hired the drivers, modified and maintained the cars that Alfa Romeo provided and managed the entire racing effort. Those Alfas had an additional serial number stamped on the frame with the prefix SF. They also carried his emblem on the body, the Prancing Horse of Maranello. Ferrari was independent, yet so closely associated with Alfa Romeo that he seemed to be an extension of the company. In his own shops he conceived and built one of the most incredibly successful racecars of all time. The engine, designed by Colombo, an Alfa Romeo engineer, was a 1.5 liter (93 cu in.) straight eight with a two-stage supercharger that ultimately produced 425 hp! Ferrari sold the car and the parts to build three more cars for Alfa Romeo. I read that they were actually buried in the ground to hide and protect them from being destroyed in the war. They simply dominated racing after World War II. Over four seasons they won thirty-one of the thirty-five events they entered, an all-time record. The cars were later known as the Alfetta Type 158.

After Enzo Ferrari severed the relationship with Alfa Romeo in 1939, he built machine tools. His workshops were bombed out twice, but the end of the war found him with new workshops and the latest equipment at Maranello, near where he was born. The first racecars Enzo Ferrari built beginning in 1947 were very small and lightweight, with the first of the V-12 engines designed by Ferrari's old friend, Gioacchino Colombo, who left Alfa Romeo and joined him at Maranello. This engine of only 1.5 liter displacement was to run with a supercharger for Grand Prix events or normally aspirated for sports car races. These models were known as the 125s (125cc × 12 cylinders = 1.5 liters). To remain competitive, the engine had to be bored out for larger displacement. The second series, therefore, were the Type 166 car. Only a few were built. Ferrari built nothing but racecars in those early years and depended on winning to support his racing passion. He was successful enough that his pride and ego grew to match his passion. He was truly an artist!

David Roth of Newport Beach advertised a little Ferrari Barchetta with no instruments, engine or gearbox and a rear axle that had been modified with a quick-change differential. By removing a plate on the differential housing, one could quickly change a set of spur gears to give different ratios for different racing circuits. The body was by Scaglietti and was obviously a later design. I bought it while I was visiting my mother and brother Walter in nearby Santa Ana. I paid $2,400 for it, knowing the body alone would cost more than that to build.

Mr. Roth had purchased it from John Horvath in Costa Mesa, but curiously, said he knew very little of its early history. He knew that it was originally equipped with a two-liter engine that had been sold to Carl Bross, and that it had been shipped back to Italy in the mid–1950s to be rebodied by Scaglietti. It obviously had been used for racing because that was the only purpose for which these cars were originally built. He thought the car had always been in California. I wrote to the factory again to ask for the history of the car but never received a reply.

I wrote to Dick Merritt and Stan Nowak, both Ferrari experts, who verified it was the sixth type 166 built, and that the original engine number was #0010M and that the engine still existed, being kept as a spare for an ex–Le Mans car. Years later I learned that Briggs Cunningham brought the first Ferrari to America, a 166 Corsa Spyder #0016, and that Jim Kimberly owned #0010M. These young men were both heirs to industrial fortunes, Cunningham from sugar and Kimberly from paper tissues. Both were very serious racing drivers. Ferrari chassis numbers at the time were two digits higher than the engine number; i.e., chassis #0012 and engine #0010 were originally together. I tried to buy the original engine, but the owner thought it had always been a spare for his car. I could not convince him otherwise and he refused to sell the engine for my car "at any price." I spent about a year trying to find another type 166 engine and gearbox. I finally bought a transmission and differential with the ring and pinion gear, but never found a proper engine. I reluctantly decided that if I was ever going to finish the car we had to resort to a later engine and gearbox.

In my search for Ferrari parts I had become acquainted with Pete Civati, an Italian born Ferrari mechanic in Santa Monica. He had an excellent, low-mileage engine and transmission from a 1964 Lusso Berlinetta Ferrari. The car had been damaged in a collision and fire, but the fire never reached the engine. Just before the accident it had been treated to a new set of valves, valve guides and the new valve guide seals, first introduced in 1965 for the 330 GT engines. As I have explained before, all Ferrari engines built before the 330GT smoked when started because no guide seals were used. This would be my first Ferrari engine that did not smoke. I also got the entire headers, exhaust and muffler system from the Lusso.

An interesting side story comes to mind. When I went to see Pete Civati about this engine, he had a gorgeous 1957 250 Testa Rossa (Red Head) competition Ferrari in his tiny showroom, right on Highway 101 in Santa Monica. The 250 Testa Rossa was the last and most powerful iteration of the Colombo designed 3-liter engine. Equipped with six two-choke Weber carburetors, it developed 300 horsepower! The huge gas tank filled the entire tail of the car. I was really impressed by how the aluminum gas tank was built with aircraft-type riveted construction, the heads of which almost touched, in absolutely perfect alignment. I wondered why they had not simply welded the tank joints, but I was sure there was a reason, probably that it had been tried and failed in racing.

Pete Civati wanted me to drive the car, but I didn't dare take it out onto that busy highway. I bought it nonetheless, for $11,000, giving Pete my check for $1,000 and an agreement that I would wire the rest when I returned home. When I got home, Jackie told me I had a call from Chris Cord. That name seemed familiar to me from my years in the neon sign business in Orange County. I seemed to recall that it was somehow connected to Richfield Oil Company. I also knew that the Cord family had something to do with founding San Clemente. I wondered who he was and why he would be calling me. When I returned his call, he began by saying that I had bought his Testa Rossa out from under him, that he had intended to buy the car from Pete Civati. He also said that he knew what I had paid for it, and asked if I would sell it to him for $15,000 and thus I would not have to ship the car home. He would pick it up from Pete. I told him that I really wanted to own the car for a while, to experience driving a real competition sports-racing car. He kept going up on his offer and I kept saying no, until the offer reached $17,000. I thought, after all, making a profit of $6,000 on a car on which I had only made a $1,000 deposit was not bad. I took his offer and when I got his check for $7,000 I called

Pete Civati with the Ferrari Testa Rossa I bought but never got to drive.

Pete Civati, and told him to let Chris buy the car for the $10,000 balance I owed.

I still wish I had been able to drive that car for a while. But even more, I wish that I had brought it home and locked it up somewhere in a vault. In 1989, when the Japanese were trying very hard to spend all the U.S. dollars they had, a Japanese collector paid $14 million for a 250 Testa Rossa! It might have been "my" car, for all I know! But the price for a Testa Rossa has gone down now. They are only worth about $7 million, last I heard.

But I digress. We had no trouble installing the 250 GT Lusso engine and transmission in the chassis because the Colombo engine was the same basic size and weight, whether it was the 1.5-Liter or the 3-liter. The original type 166 engine had produced 140 horsepower, but this 1964 GT engine produced 250 horsepower, without adding any weight, or changing the balance and weight distribution of the car. Although we had bought a type 166 five-speed transmission and rear differential, we chose to use the Lusso's all synchronized transmission and Halibrand quick-change differential.

The 1949 Type 166 Ferrari with the 1954 Scaglietti Barchetta body.

We changed the spur gears to give a 3.62: 1 overall ratio and an estimated top speed of 160 mph at the engine's 7200 rpm limit.

We realized that the little car was not likely to be driven at anything like that top speed, but it had a surplus of power compared to the original engine, and we believed this gear ratio choice would result in a more practical and safe performance. This little car was very lightweight. We did not weigh it, but we estimated it was about 1900 pounds dry weight.

This beautiful little all aluminum body was built over a very light steel tubing frame. The covered headlights and Plexiglas windscreen added to the simple, elegant lines of the body. The faired-in headrest and the sturdy chrome-plated roll bar offered some protection in case of a rollover. The roll bar may have been original, or added by Scaglietti, for there were tube sockets provided in the car's chassis frame into which the roll bar fit.

No instruments came with the car and after a prolonged and fruitless search, we settled for installing a set of Veglia instruments from an Alfa Romeo. There was no trim at all on the inside of the cockpit, merely flat black paint. The seats appeared to be the original buckets, with big racing-type seat belts.

The hood and "trunk" lids were not hinged. They hooked into slots at the front and were held into place by spring-loaded clamps with big finger-loops to pull and rotate them to lift the panels off entirely for service, or to fill the huge gas tank that barely left room for the spare mounted on top of the tank.

Our choice of gear ratios proved to be about right. This little car, with about the same horsepower as my 250MMs, proved to be almost as fast. I never was able to time either of them accurately. Although I had Brian ride with me with a stopwatch, trying to get a zero to sixty time, I was never willing to race the engine and pop the clutch as would be necessary to get the fastest time. I was too simpatico with my cars.

The cockpit with Veglia Alfa instruments.

I was fortunate to live in the country where I could drive these cars pretty fast, yet safely. I used to feel sorry for people that lived in a big city who owned a horse, a good hunting dog or a Ferrari. By contrast I had that little up-hill corkscrew turn I have previously referred to, and beyond that, my road dead-ended on a good two-lane state highway with lots of curves going around a big lake. A few miles further was my favorite, long sweeping curve, so well banked that it could be taken at almost any speed as long as you kept the pedal down. It was in farm country with very little traffic and no intersections, and it was hard to resist driving a car like this quite fast. I hope there is a statute of limitations for speeding. If not, I may have to spend my last years in jail. I hasten to add, however, that I was never a careless or reckless driver. If other cars were anywhere in sight, I drove at the normal, legal speeds.

At my home on the outskirts of Fort Collins.

I advertised the Type 166 for sale in 1974, and when I had no takers, I took it to Tom Barrett's auction in Scottsdale. I was always leery of car auctions. Those by English auction companies are at least dignified, but those held by American companies were more like a carnival sideshow. The only difference, it seemed to me, was they didn't wear clown outfits. The car didn't bring my reserve price, but I sold it after the auction to Joe Marchetti, a restaurateur cum Ferrari dealer in Chicago. At least he paid my $14,000 price and appreciated what the car had once been.

I hoped that at some point the little 166 would be reunited with its original engine, number 0010M. If it were to be, and if the Ferrari historians sorted out the entire history of this very early Ferrari, it would have great value.

Indeed they have; John Hopfenbeck of Burlingame, California, is just such an historian. He kindly sent me the following history of this little Ferrari Barchetta: It had an impressive racing history in the first four years of its life. Roberto Vallone of Rome was the original owner. Vallone and Sighinolfi drove it in the 1949 Mille Miglia, not finishing. They also drove it in the 1949 Targa Florio. Vallone drove it in the 1949 San Remo F1 Gran Prix to eighth overall, the '49 Marsseille GP to eighth overall, the '49 F2 GP at Bari (Italy) to fifth overall, the '49 GP of Naples, first overall. It was driven to first overall by Vallone and Meloni in the '49 Giro dell'Umbria and the '49 Coppa d'Oro delle Dolomiti. Vallone then competed in hillclimb races in 1949. It passed on to Emilio Romana, who drove it in the 1951 Mille Miglia to 38th overall. And it ran again in the Mille Miglia in 1952, not finishing, driven by Guarducci and Bianco. Several years later it turned up in Costa Mesa, California, owned by John Horvath, who sold the engine 0010M to Carl Bross in 1968. It then passed on to David Roth, then to me. Joe Marchetti sold it to Ed Niles in 1976 who sold it to Bob Lloyd of Justin, TX, and then in 1978 it went to Bob Taylor. One of these men paid $46,000 for the original gearbox and engine, #0010M, finally making the car whole again. Jon Baumgartner of Los Altos, California, owned it in '83, and then it went to Jean Pierre Slavic of Geneva. It was shown in 2000, rebodied by Dino Cognolato in a style resembling its original body. This tends to prove that we never really own these cars—we are merely stewards to whom the car is entrusted.

Note: The Testa Rosa that I "owned" for a couple of days but never brought home or drove is now worth as much as $14,000,000! And the properly restored 166 Barchetta, with its original engine, is now worth $1,700,000.

16

The Alfa Romeo Disco Volante

During the late '20's and '30s Luigi Fusi worked in the drafting department of Alfa Romeo under the great Vittorio Jano, the chief engineer who designed the outstanding pre-war supercharged GP and sports-racing Alfa Romeos. When Luigi Fusi retired he was made curator of the Alfa museum.

The 1953 Alfa Romeo Disco Volante (Flying Saucer).

He wrote a book in Italian, with English sidebars, that covered every Alfa Romeo built since 1910. The book was invaluable to me, or anyone interested in Alfa history or the basic technical specifications of every model ever built. Illustrations of every production model were included as well as many photographs of one-off show cars built by Italy's finest Carrozzerie.

In 1952, Alfa had built two new engines upon which Alfa's future production cars were to be based. The new four-cylinder engines were put into several very low and wide custom-built roadsters. Since this was the age of flying saucer sightings, Alfa Romeo called them Disco Volante, or Flying Saucer. One six-cylinder car was built with that body style. It was that engine that was further developed into the 3000CM competition cars, all with ultra light coupe bodies hammered out by Colli. Even though their shape had changed, the nickname Disco Volante stuck with the racing crowd. Only five of these cars were built. Juan Fangio drove this car to second place in the '53 Mille Miglia, with the left front wheel flapping because of a broken tie rod. None finished at Le Mans. They were all retired at the end of the '53 season. This car was turned over to Pininfarina to use as a styling platform on which he built several dream cars. First was the Super Flow with up-swing windows, then Super Flow II, then a roadster and finally this car. All of them were actually the same body, rebuilt with very advanced styling for that era. This car was the last one.

In the February 1961 issue of *Sports Car Illustrated*, Karl Ludvigsen wrote an article entitled "Last of the Red-Hot Alfas" that filled my heart and mind with pure lust. Oh, I would love to have that car! As a professional designer I was always interested in good styling and engineering, and I felt that the Italians led the world in both at that time, first expressed through the Alfa Romeos then through the beautiful Ferraris. Ludvigsen's article was about the last Pininfarina show car I had seen in Fusi's book. But it was what was under the skin of the car that thrilled me the most. That glamorous body was built on one of the five competition cars built in 1953 to compete in the Mille Miglia and Le Mans, and it was never detuned!

You can imagine my surprise to discover that Howard Wignall of Littleton, a suburb of Denver, owned that very car. The Disco Volante had made a tour of the U.S. Alfa dealers to promote sales, and at the end of the tour it was left with Continental Alfa in Boulder. Howard Wignall was the first registered owner. I immediately opened a dialog with the hope of buying it. I had no idea what a car like that might be worth, but Ludvigsen wrote that it had cost $40,000 to build in 1953 ($290,000 now).

After I had convinced Mr. Wignall I was serious about buying the car, he and his wife drove it to Fort Collins to meet Jackie and me for lunch

The double-overhead cam engine with six Webers and ram-air intake.

at the Holiday Inn, off I-25. He had just retired and they wanted to build a new home in Estes Park where he would pursue wildlife photography. He wanted $35,000 for it. Bob Sutherland was also interested in the car, and offered to trade lumber for it. Howard did not allow me to drive it then, but it only had about 7,000 miles on the odometer. They took the car home, and I began planning how to raise that much cash. I asked if he was interested in taking one of my cars in trade. At that time I already had about $100,000 invested in cars ($340,000 in cheap 2005 dollars). I asked if he could take something in trade, but he wanted cash. We finally reached an agreement whereby I would pay him $20,000 down and pay the balance as I could spare the cash, at 5 percent interest, for no longer than two years. That's the only time I bought a collectible car without paying cash for it. I raised the $20,000 by selling the Targa Florio Mercedes to Bob Sutherland, on a contract, and assigning the contract to my bank.

I drove it home to get the feel of the car, and it was simply fantastic. The only cars that were as thrilling for me to drive were the 8C-2.3, the 8C 2.9 Alfas and the 250 Mille Miglia Ferraris. The acceleration felt like a big spring was being released. It was also more comfortable than any high performance car I had driven up to that time. The sliding Plexiglas roof panels looked great but generated so much solar heat that it was impossible to drive with them closed when the sun was out. When slightly open, the car was pleasant, with not much wind.

For anyone interested in a detailed technical description of the car, find a copy of Ludvigsen's article. The drawing in the article shows the layout, with a backbone type space frame, independent de Dion rear suspension with coil springs around big tube shocks, and double wishbone and coil springs and shocks on the front. The 3.5-liter engine develops 270 hp at 6500 rpm, with six side-draft Weber 48DOM carburetors. Steering is precise with just 2⅓ turns lock to lock. The five-speed transmission is a non-synchronized racing box with dog clutches and can be speed shifted up or down even without the clutch when the engine speed is equalized just right. The shift lever was mounted on the very high, carpeted tunnel and it felt solid as a bank vault.

The gearing is out of this world for high-speed road racing. Speed through the gears is 66, 93, 122, 145 and 166! And the drum brakes were the best I have ever experienced, and may have been the most advanced drum brakes ever. They would bring the car down fast and smoothly. The rear brakes were inboard to reduce unsprung weight and stress on the outer half-shafts. The front brakes were 4.5" wide, with two shoes side by side. I put the car over the pit in my garage at home, and just marveled at the beautiful drive train and undercarriage. Howard Wignall had carefully cleaned and hand-painted most of the frame members and linkage. I completed what he had not yet done.

And all this was designed and built in 1953! With just 213 cubic inches and only 8.2 to 1 compression ratio! At the same time, with 9 to 1 compression ratio, Ferrari was getting 240 hp out of the 1953 three liter V-12 Mille Miglia roadsters. Marzotto, a Mille Miglia specialist, won the race driving a Ferrari with the big 4.5-liter V-12 engine, but Fangio would surely have won if the tie rod had not broken. Had Alfa Romeo chosen to further develop and improve the reliability of these cars, they might have been one of the greatest road-racing cars Alfa ever built. Even though this show-car body was much heavier than the super light Colli coupe bodies built for racing, it would still fly!

After driving the car on the county roads around Fort Collins, I decided to accept an invitation to drive it in the third annual 1976 Historic Races at Laguna Seca, near Carmel, California. I had never driven in any sort of competition before, but Steve Earle assured me that this was not serious racing, and that I would be given some circuit driving time with an instructor before the race. These vintage cars were becoming very valuable and no one wanted to wreck their cars.

I had purchased a used truck with an enclosed body for the car shop. To prepare the Disco Volante for the race our son Brian drove the truck with the Disco to Wichita, Kansas, to Alf Francis, the former chief mechanic for the British ALTA racing team. He would change all the fluids and filters, adjust the timing and install carburetor jets for running at sea level, and generally inspect the car. Unfortunately, the beautiful nose of the car was damaged in transporting it, so Brian came back empty, and I flew to Wichita to pick the car up when it was repaired. Driving the car home from Wichita would allow me to be much more familiar with its handling before I drove it in the race.

I knew I could not drive fast on I-70 across Kansas, which is well patrolled. I had received more than one ticket in Kansas just traveling on business. I took the secondary roads in Kansas, working my way from Wichita in the southern part to Highway 36 near the top of the state. These were all two-lane highways, but carried very little traffic, and I came through on a Sunday. There are a lot of wide-open spaces in upper Kansas and eastern Colorado. I was able to drive safely as fast as I wanted on some stretches without worrying about traffic and cops. I entered Colorado after dark, and was driving comfortably at over 100 miles and hour. At one gas stop, I thought I had better check the big dry-sump oil tank in the engine compartment, and was amazed that it was down about a gallon! Then I recalled the 2.9 Alfa dry-sump engine had used an amazing amount of oil on a similar trip. These racing engines have a lot of valve-stem clearance in the guides to ensure adequate lubrication and avoid the risk of valves sticking. I dumped in a gallon of 40-weight Castrol and continued home on Highway 34, a total of almost 500 miles. I was now very familiar with the car and what it would do.

Brian and his wife, JoAnn, drove the truck with the Disco to Laguna Seca and stayed for the races. I drove Jackie with our daughter Barbara and her husband Tom Haynie to see the races too. Bob Sutherland and his wife were there with the Targa Florio Mercedes, but would run in a different race. After we unloaded the Disco Volante, it attracted a lot of attention, and Phil Hill, America's first Grand Prix champion driver, came by to see it. I introduced myself and told him that it was the car Fangio drove in the '53 Mille Miglia, but I think he was dubious. I asked him if he would be interested in driving it in the race instead of me, but he declined.

I had two practice sessions of about five or six laps each with an instructor. He showed me how to place the car on the apex of the curves. The track has been changed now, I believe, but then it was about two miles around, with nine turns. There was a tight corkscrew bend that was the most difficult for me, and there was a very slow, tight turn before the cars went up a long, uphill straight. The start and finish line was around the middle of that long straight. For whatever reason, I was on the inside of the tenth and last row. This made me think it was because I was a first-time rank amateur driver. Then I looked to see Phil Hill on my right, driving Briggs Cunningham's D-Type Jag. Several times we were told not to get carried away, that this was just for fun. Like hell it was! When the flag dropped those professionals in the front rows driving factory prepared

Coming out of the "Corkscrew" at Laguna Seca. My family watched from here.

D-Jaguars may not have been racing all-out, but they sure set a very fast pace, and Phil Hill took off after eighteen cars in front of us. I had to make a split-second decision to toddle along in the rear or try to keep up. So I tried to keep up with Phil.

I must say that I have never concentrated so intently on anything in my life. I drove the car as hard and as fast as I possibly could while still keeping it well under control, and also watching the other drivers around me. I started passing cars too, and I passed six in the first two laps, mostly on the long straight. I was not far behind Phil Hill's car. With the tall gearing on my car, the whole race was run in first and second gear except for shifting into third gear near the end of the long straight, only to brake for turn one, downshift and accelerate to turn two. The corkscrew must have been about turn seven, and you came out of it on a sweeping S curve towards the tight turn 9. Jackie, Brian, JoAnn, Barbara and Tom were on the hillside overlooking the downhill just beyond the corkscrew. Barbara was so excited she was jumping up and down, yelling to me, but I could hear nothing over the Alfa's great roar when driven hard. The un-muffled exhaust came out on the left side, away from the driver, just in front of the rear tire.

This was a ten lap race, but on the sixth lap, as I was accelerating hard on the uphill straight, the clutch began to slip. I had never driven the car this hard, and Alf Francis had no place to test it. It had a twin-plate clutch that must have been set up with less pressure to make driving on the street easier. Moreover, once it began to slip, the twin discs began to heat and warp and slipped even more. I raised my left arm to signal I was pulling to the right edge of the course, and nursed it through the hairpin, turn nine and into the pits. I let the clutch cool and could then drive the car so long as I did not apply too much power. Not finishing was a huge disappointment for me. I later told Jackie that I had never had so much fun in my life!

I was pleasantly surprised when a gentleman asked if I would be willing to exhibit the Disco Volante on the lawn at Pebble Beach the next day. We did, which was another first for us. This annual Concours d'Élégance at Pebble Beach was already established as the premier event in America, if not the world. I hastened to acquiesce!

After Brian brought the car home I wrote to Luigi Fusi, who had the factory make a new clutch assembly to the original specifications (for no charge), and Loran installed it. I had the car for almost three years, and drove it frequently. It never failed to give me a thrill to experience the smooth power on a fast drive in the country. Eventually I decided to sell it and placed a nice display ad in *Hemmings*, with three views of the car.

Bob Sutherland was a great enthusiast. He had been buying sports-racing cars from time to time, and now had a fine collection of very rare and desirable automobiles. He kept his collection in a nice metal building he had built on the back of his residential property. He also was instrumental in founding a car club in Denver and the Colorado Grand. I joined but only went a couple of times to see what he had added. He was interested in the Disco Volante but the timing wasn't right.

Ernest Kanzler bought the car in February of 1979 for $40,000. I had met Ernest about ten years earlier. He owned an 8C-2.6 Alfa MM roadster that he demonstrated by taking me for a wild ride through the Hollywood hills where he had a beautiful home. I had kept in touch with letters, hoping he might want to sell his Alfa at some time. When we first met Ernest told me that his grandfather had been associated with Henry Ford regarding the acquisition of Lincoln. Ernest had also worked for Ford in the styling department. Judging by what little I saw of his life-style he was apparently very wealthy.

When he came to our home to pick up the Alfa, he was wearing a full-length nutria fur coat. We went into my small office where I expected Ernest to write a check for the $40,000 for the car. Instead, he opened that huge coat, zipped open a large inside pocket and put a pile of $100 bills on my desk, still in their wrappers, and asked me to count out what I needed. I called Jackie into the office to help me count 400 $100 bills while Ernest looked at my car pictures on the wall. When we finished counting, there were still a number of unopened bundles of bills. I suggested he should recount it to be sure we were correct, but Ernest just said, "That's OK" and returned the unopened bundles to his coat pocket. Even though it was mid-winter and the Disco had no heater, after visiting his son at CU in Boulder, he drove the car back to California. He wrote to say he had a blast! He had moved to Costa Mesa, where he had a twenty-car collection, but his 8C Alfa was out of commission with a blown engine. I saw it hanging from the rafters of his building when I visited him on a trip to see my mother, who lived in Santa Ana. By then, Ernest had started to build the Kanzler, a good-looking sports car of his own design, but very few were ever built.

In about 1985 I went to Friday Harbor because Ernie called to tell me he was selling his cars and I could have the 8C-2.6 MM Alfa for $150,000 if I wanted it. I was restoring two Alfas at the time and could not afford another one so I tried to help Peter Giddings buy the car by going to Friday Harbor to see it. My wife, her sister Betty and her husband Bob Braas were with us. Bob had been in the marine hardware business in Seattle most of his working life, and to say that he was very careful with his considerable money would be an understatement. He made a Scotsman look like a spendthrift. When Bob saw the derelict Alfa, with parts in boxes, he was incredulous. He could not believe anyone would pay $150,000 for such a pile of junk!

Ernest had never rebuilt the Alfa and it was in very sorry condition. Apparently the word got out that Ernest was going to sell the Alfa. Suddenly Peter Giddings was bidding against Chris Mann from England, his arch-competitor in racing. Peter had sent a bank draft for $150,000 if Ernest would accept it but out of nowhere, Peter and Chris were both outbid by Californian Don Orosco, who put it up for sale soon after. Burkhard von Schenk purchased it, shipped it to England and had Paul Grist completely restore it and correct the modified bodywork. With its known racing history, even with a non-original Monza engine, it would be worth at least $2,500,000 now.

The Disco Volante that I had sold him was also there in Ernest's storage building. Like the old Alfa it was also out of commission with the heads off the engine. The Disco Volante was subsequently sold to someone in England. Wherever it is now, I hope it is in the good hands of someone who takes care of it and enjoys driving it as much as I did. It must be, for

Ernest Kanzler's 8C-2.6-liter Alfa, no. 2211126, partly dismantled.

the car was featured in the English magazine *Classic and Sports Car* in April 1989, in a story titled "Flying Sorcery."

Ernest Kanzler was one of the most interesting and colorful people I have met though my automobile machinations. The last time I saw him was on Friday Island in the Juan de Fuca Straits, in about 1993. He had moved there and owned a large farm on the island where he had a stable of expensive Arabian horses. Ernest was also rebuilding a 100-foot long tugboat and was equipping it with electronic controls so that he could sail it by himself, without a crew. He said he wanted to take it around the world. He had a large crew of people working on the tug in the harbor. When I saw him, he wore a beard, with his long blond hair in a ponytail. I would love to know if he finished the boat, and if so what happened to him after that.

The 6000CM "Disco Volante" is too rare to have an established value, but I guess it would be at least $1 million.

17

The 1930 6C-1750
Alfa Romeo Zagato Spider

After I became interested in the 8C 2.3 Alfas, when I was in Chicago on business I usually took time to visit Keith Hellon in nearby Mundelein. It was always a pleasure for me to spend time with Keith. When we first met he owned a long chassis 8C-2.3 Alfa with a Brianza body. After selling my first 8C Alfa I continued to look for another unrestored Alfa that I could afford. Keith sold his 8C Alfa and soon began restoring supercharged Alfas full time in a barn-like building he rented out in the country. He usually had several of his customers' cars there, and I worried about a fire or theft, but neither ever happened. At today's values, they would be worth millions of dollars.

Keith had acquired a 1930 fourth series Gran Sport short chassis 6C-1750 Zagato with matching chassis and engine numbers, #8513064. It also had most of its original Zagato body, #2818, which was an important factor in its value, even though it was not complete. It was missing its lower louvered hood panels and some of the fenders, the aluminum battery boxes, the headlights, taillights and the top bows that normally were folded and stored inside the compartment behind the seats. The car, already over forty years old, needed a full restoration. These light aluminum bodies were originally formed by highly skilled craftsmen beating the aluminum panels to shape, usually over sand-bags or forms. This work-hardens the aluminum, and with years of driving and probable racing when they were new, the aluminum fatigues and begins to crack. Very few of the 8C and 6C Alfas had their original bodies, and a totally original body is very rare today.

Keith had only started the engine work, and just as we did, he farmed out the engine machine work. He had the crankshaft ground and the babbitt rod and main bearings poured and bored. Keith needed some cash so in February of 1974 I bought the car for $8,500—$3,500 in cash plus a very nice 1967 Aston Martin Volante convertible coupe that I purchased from my brother for $5,000. I sent my son-in-law, Sam Haugland, to pick it up.

The six cylinder Alfas were much less desirable and valuable than the 8C cars; nevertheless this was the first unmodified supercharged Alfa I had found that I was able to buy, and I resolved to do our very best to make it as perfect a restoration as possible. Ron Kerr began work on the engine and dismantling the rest of the car for sandblasting, painting and rebuilding all the components. Sam Haugland had recently married our youngest daughter, Jennifer. Sam was a musician and since his jobs were at night, he worked almost full time for me at my sign company. I put him to work dismantling, cataloging and storing parts, sandblasting those parts that were steel, dismantling the wire-spoked wheels, and cleaning the aluminum parts.

Ron Kerr left my company that spring, and not much was done until I hired Loran Swanson in the fall. We had two other cars in progress at

The restored 1930 6C-1750 Zagato Alfa Romeo at my home.

the time, and I wanted the Alfa work done to perfection, so it took several years to finish this Alfa. Also, there was a lot of delay waiting for parts. I had a new stainless steel exhaust and muffler system made in England to match the original from drawings I made. I sent all the instruments to England to be rebuilt and fitted with new faces. We had the six wheels rebuilt with chrome-plated rims and stainless steel spokes. I ordered new Dunlop tires and tubes.

A big problem was the radiator, which had serious leaks. The original radiator cores were hand-made from brass square tubes about 8mm in size. These tubes were stacked, with copper wire spacers between each row, horizontally and vertically, like a honeycomb, and then saw-cut to fit the core size needed. Then the outside and inside faces of the pre-assembled square tube core were dipped into a shallow pan of molten solder, just enough to seal the spaces between the tubes to a depth of about one-eighth inch. This left the space around each square tube throughout the core for water circulation. Neither the 8C nor the 6C Alfas had a radiator fan. They depended on these very efficient radiators and the ribbed aluminum oil pans for dissipating the engine heat. But the radiators were easily damaged by flying stones, especially if the car had been raced on unpaved roads. Also, the outer radiator shell was chrome plated and was soldered directly to the core on the inside of the shell. We shipped the radiator to a specialist to repair it. To protect the precious radiator, I made a pattern of the outer shape of the radiator and sent it to another specialist to have a chrome-plated wire-mesh stone guard made. Many Alfas had used stone guards originally, but none came with my car.

I managed to borrow a set of original top bows, by posting a large cash bond to guarantee their safe and prompt return, and Loran made exact duplicates for my car. Also the Bosch headlights that were used originally were no longer manufactured, but I found that Bosch, in Germany, could still provide the next generation of headlights that were very similar in shape and fit the same stanchions as the originals. They were also very good 12-volt lights. We had to make the taillights, matching the originals as closely as possible.

Loran finished the engine first. These 6C Alfas had double overhead camshafts with a gearwheel on the rear end of each camshaft. These were turned by means of spiral-beveled gears at the top of a vertical shaft, with another set of gears at the bottom of the shaft, driven off the crankshaft. This shaft drive system made it very critical that the backlash clearance on these gears was precise. This in turn made the align boring critical as well as any milling of the head or the top of the engine block equally critical. Any material machined away from the head or block, or the center-

The supercharged intake side and the six-branch exhaust side.

ing of the main bearing bores, affected the alignment of the camshaft drive gears. Loran had no previous experience with a 6C Alfa engine, and Keith Hellon had already done the align boring of the main bearings. Although we didn't know it then, the end result was that there was not quite enough clearance on the camshaft drive gears. The engine ran well, but would likely cause trouble later.

The rest of the restoration presented no special problems that we had not faced before. The transmission gears were badly worn. I had made contact with A.F.R.A., a firm in Italy that was the parts concessionaire for obsolete Alfa parts. They supplied a complete new set of transmission gears for $1165 in 1981 dollars ($2500 in today's dollars). Every component of the car was done as perfectly as we could make it, and the finished car was beautiful! I drove the car enough to seat the rings and tune the engine. It ran well for me.

There were no mechanical or electric fuel pumps on these cars. The black tank on the firewall was a vacuum tank that fed the carburetor by gravity. As the fuel level in that tank went down, a float-valve opened a vacuum line from the engine and the fuel from the regular gas tank was thereby sucked into the vacuum tank. Most cars of that vintage used vacuum tanks.

Except for photographs in Luigi Fusi's book I had never seen a photo of a Zagato with the top up. The top bows were made to fold up enough to store the top in the small compartment behind the seats, covered with a snap-on canvas cover. Most of these tops were simply removed and were seldom used again. The instruments were under the cowl, and hard to see. I had to duck my head down if I wanted to see the tachometer or speedometer.

Seven years after I bought the car, in January of 1981, I advertised the

A rare picture of an Alfa Romeo Zagato with the top up.

There were no bumpers on an Alfa and I had to duck to see the instruments.

Zagato in a full-page illustrated display ad in *Hemmings Motor News*. These cars had been going up in value quite rapidly. I sold the car to Tom Perkins for $100,000, which is equal to a little over $200,000 in today's inflated dollars. I made a substantial profit at the time. Tom Perkins was then a

The finished interior.

wealthy California investment banker and was investing in supercharged vintage cars. We did not meet in person, as our transaction was by phone and wire transfer of funds. One of my employees delivered the car in my covered van. When it came to his home Tom called to tell me how satisfied he was, that it was everything I had represented it to be in our phone discussions. I was pleased too, for I was proud of the restoration we had done.

Meanwhile, I had purchased another 6C-1750 as a total basket case, and I had finally found another 8C-2.3 Alfa Romeo. Loran was working exclusively on those two cars at the time I sold the Zagato to Tom Perkins. I finished the 8C-2.3 car in 1983 and I contacted Tom Perkins as a potential buyer. I was surprised when Perkins told me he was now unhappy with the 6C Zagato because Phil Reilly, who is a highly regarded engine and mechanical restoration expert in California, had told him the engine was poorly done. After owning the car for two years, Perkins wanted me to take the car back. He said that I had knowingly sold the car with a poorly rebuilt engine. Now, if there is anything I valued more than Alfas, it was my reputation as an honest man. I told Tom that I did not have the cash to refund his money, but that I would take the car back as soon as I sold

Phil Reilly working his magic on my 6C-1750 Engine.

the 8C Alfa. He wanted to come to Colorado with Phil Reilly to see the 8C Alfa with the intent of buying it and returning the six-cylinder Alfa in trade.

I had never met Phil Reilly, but I certainly knew of him and respected him as one of the best specialists for vintage and high-performance engines in the United States. Tom Perkins and Phil Reilly came to my home to see the now completed 8C 2.3 Alfa (which is the subject of a later chapter). Phil assured me that there really were problems in the cam drive gear mesh of the 6C Alfa Zagato, and although there had not been any catastrophic damage, the engine needed to be done properly. I found Phil Reilly to be a very modest, unassuming man, in spite of his enviable reputation as a genius with engines. This situation put him in a rather embarrassing situation. Tom Perkins owned the very nice building that housed Phil's impeccable shop facility, and it also housed Tom Perkins' small collection of supercharged cars that Phil looked after for Perkins. Tom Perkins had published a small book dealing with his very exclusive collection of prewar supercharged cars. Both Alfa Romeos featured in his book were formerly mine. In addition, he had an SSK Mercedes, a Type 57 SC Bugatti. He also had a rare British Squire, the engine of which was an almost exact copy of the 8C Alfa, so close in fact, Squire only made a few before Alfa threatened legal action.

The 8C-2.3 Alfa was finished cosmetically and mechanically to a very high standard, but Phil expressed some concern about the engine because of the gear problem he had found in the 6C engine. I had to assume his comments about the 8C engine were to give Tom Perkins a bargaining chip. The 8C engine is entirely different, without the type of camshaft drive that was a rather notorious problem for the six cylinder cars. Moreover, we had rebuilt my first 8C Alfa and were very familiar with these engines and I knew we had rebuilt it properly. Tom Perkins and Phil Reilly took the 8C Alfa for a drive. I told them of my favorite roads where they could drive the car hard. They were gone for almost an hour. When they returned Tom Perkins said he would buy my car at my asking price if I would take the 6C back for what he paid for it, so Perkins paid an additional $65,000 for the 8C-2.3 Alfa. I had hoped to keep this Alfa and I was not very happy about all this, but my integrity was at stake.

Rather than ship the Zagato back to Colorado, I asked if Phil would re-do the engine for me. I told him I wanted it rebuilt to be safe for vintage racing, and that I was not concerned about anything other than the engine since I knew what we had done to the rest of the car. As usual, I put no cost constraints on Phil to do the engine, and even though he gave me an hourly rate that was somewhat less than he usually charged his affluent clientele, it was expensive. Phil found and fixed all the problems in the cam-drive system and did anything else that he thought needed attention for it to be safe for vintage racing. I visited his shop several times in the course of about eighteen months. I asked them to test drive the car, and because the car had sat for so long, the carburetor needed attention.

I received another invitation to drive the 6C Alfa in the vintage races at Laguna Seca in 1985, the "Year of the Alfa." The Alfa factory was sending over one of their great type 158 Grand Prix cars to be driven in an exhibition by none other than Juan Fangio, five times Grand Prix World Champion. Other world champions would be there too, including Phil Hill. I had intended to drive my Alfa personally, but it occurred to me that I would rather see Phil Hill drive it if he was willing to do so. I had left the car in California with my friend, Peter Giddings, in Walnut Creek. I drove the Alfa down to Laguna Seca on the Interstate, while Jackie followed in our car. That was a pretty hairy ride.

The traffic was horrible, and a lot of cars kept trying to get close enough to see what the Alfa was, including a lot of semi-truck drivers, who sometimes had me sandwiched in between! I was really glad to get off that highway and to the Laguna Seca circuit.

I located Phil Hill and asked him to drive my car. He was reluctant because he said he had had previous bad experiences with other people's cars and he didn't want to risk damaging mine. I told him that Phil Reilly had just rebuilt the engine to be raced safely and that I was confident

Phil Hill driving my Alfa on a practice lap.

The pit crew adjusting the brakes. I'm supervising from under the hat.

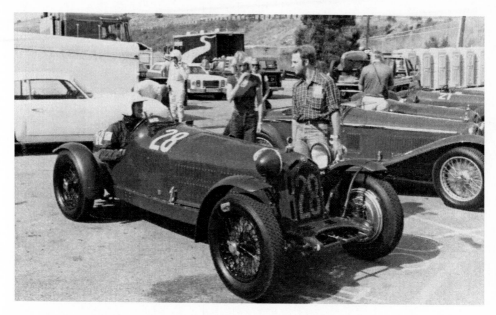

Peter Giddings in his 2.6-liter Monza Alfa. His wife Judith and John deBoer are at right.

Phil Hill, America's first Grand Prix Champion, signing autographs.

enough of the car's condition that I was willing to accept any damage that might occur. He agreed. When it came time to practice, Phil took it around the circuit a couple of times getting used to it, and when he came into the pits he said there was something wrong with the way it handled.

He asked what the tire pressures were and I told him 32 pounds, as the manual recommended. He said, "That's the problem" and had them pumped up to 55 pounds. He took it out again for a couple more laps of the circuit, and was flagged in because it was leaking water. When we checked, it was not really leaking; it had just overflowed a bit by being filled completely. The track stewards told us we had to have an overflow reservoir. I was the one-man pit crew until Dale Macgowan, the owner of Alfa West in Denver, who had been to Fort Collins with the Colorado Alfa Club to see my cars and was watching us in the pit lane, asked if he could help. I gratefully said that he and his friend were now the official pit crew. He tied a soup can under the overflow tube with some wire, and Phil did another lap. Phil had also reported a slight pull to the right when braking and Dale adjusted the right front brake shoe. Phil announced that it was now ready to race.

Before the practice laps ended, I took our daughter, Barbara, for one lap of the circuit at a pretty good clip. The crowds in the stands loved that beautiful old Alfa Romeo and we got a lot of thumbs-ups. Barbara was thrilled, and I was happy to be able to drive the circuit again. My last time was nine years previously in 1976. The Corkscrew was still there. And even at sixty-three years old, I thought I still drove pretty well.

The cars were lined up in the pits in the order in which they would start the race. In the front row were Peter Giddings and Chris Mann, the two Englishmen who were serious racing competitors, both in their much more powerful 8C Monza Alfas. Third was another 8C-Alfa and Phil Hill was fourth in the 6C Zagato. The Monza Alfas had about a seventy horsepower advantage over my Alfa, and both Peter and Chris were very good drivers. Behind Phil Hill was none other than Phil Reilly driving my old 8C-2.3 Alfa that now belonged to Tom Perkins. There were several other eight-cylinder and six-cylinder Alfas in that race. It was really exciting to watch Phil Hill, our first American Grand Prix champion, drive my little Alfa! He would go into a turn fast, waiting until the last second, then with a flick of the wrist, he would place the car into a four-wheel drift to scrub off speed and come shooting out of the turn very fast. He kept close behind the three 8C Alfa Monzas and finished the race in fourth place, just as he had started, in spite of racing against much faster Alfas. That illustrates the difference between very good drivers such as Giddings and Mann, and a world's champion like Phil Hill.

Phil drove the car around to our allotted parking area. I told him what a thrill it was for me to see him driving my car, especially those four-wheel drifts into the corners, just like Nuvolari. Phil said the pleasure was all his that he had forgotten how much fun the old Alfas were to drive. He had a 6C-1750 of his own that he had owned for many years. It was out of commission, and he said this was an incentive for him to get it rebuilt.

Before the race I had also been asked to be a judge for the Alfa Romeo Class at the Pebble Beach Concours d'Élégance the next day. I was further pleased and surprised when I was asked to exhibit the Alfa Zagato there as well. This is quite an honor, for only one of the cars that are raced at Laguna Seca is invited to do that, and mine was chosen again. My Disco Volante was chosen in 1973, the first time I came to Laguna Seca with a car.

It had been another wonderful weekend for Jackie and me and for our daughter Barbara and her husband Tom Haynie, who took the wonderful photographs reproduced here. The chief judge for the Alfas was Simon

Congratulating Phil for driving an exciting race. Tom Mudd, in white, drove his 8C Alfa.

A very tired Art Valdez finishes the 1000 Miglia in Italy.

Moore, who came from England, and besides myself there was Dr. Fred Simeone, a brain surgeon from Philadelphia who owned several Alfa Romeos, and Ivan Zaremba, of Phil Reilly & Company, who had done a lot of the work on my car.

I didn't bother to ship the Alfa home because I wanted to sell it and I knew the most likely buyer would be a Californian. The car's performance at Laguna Seca and the exposure to thousands of people at Pebble Beach would add value to the car. My being a judge for the Alfas and having Phil Reilly rebuild the engine would no doubt produce a buyer for top dollar. I stored the car at Peter Giddings' home where he had several shop buildings. I soon sold the Alfa to Art Valdez, a real estate developer in the Los Angeles area. He paid $125,000 for it and kept the car for eleven years. He had a new radiator header tank made and took it to Italy for the Mille Miglia three times. It performed well every time, I believe, which is a testimony to Phil Reilly's engine work and to the rest of the car that Loran restored.

After Art Valdez drove it in the 1986 1000 Miglia he sent me the autographed photograph shown here, taken at the finish line, with the inscription, "To Jackson, Thanks for the lovely car. It performed well and we finished. Art." Art drove it in the Mille Miglia again in 1988 and 1990. He sold the car in about 1996 to Mark Mountanos. Presently Alan Frick of California owns the Alfa.

With its provenance and the recent driving history, in perfect condition it would be worth about $700,000 today.

18

The 250 GT Boano Ferraris

Before I sold my first 250MM Ferrari in 1969, I bought a 1956 Ferrari 250GT (serial or engine number #1285) to restore. It was a Boano coupe, a style that was and is still among the lowest priced 12-cylinder early Ferraris to be had. These were among the first Ferraris designed to be series built. While the chassis frame, engine, transmission and suspension system are essentially the same as that of the 212 Inter, they have a longer wheelbase and were tuned for touring in grand style. They had a softer clutch and suspension, but the engine still turned out 240 hp at 7,000 rpm. While they were larger and heavier they would do zero to sixty in about seven seconds, which at that time was a very fast car for driving on the street.

Their low value, then and now, had nothing to do with quality or performance; it was their looks. Compared to the delectable one-off custom Ferraris that were coach-built for famous and wealthy clients, these Boano bodies were pretty plebeian. Their styling was rather plain and simple but the build quality was better than most of the earlier Ferraris. They are comparatively rare, with only 130 built from 1956 to 1958. A few had aluminum bodies. Although they were not intended for serious racing, private owners raced them with some success in GT races and the Alpine and Acropolis Rallies. They sold new for $10,500. This one needed work so I bought it from Ed Niles for only about $1,800, as I recall.

We were now quite familiar with the Ferrari and I was interested in seeing how very similar the later cars still were to the first 250MM competition cars we first rebuilt. Because none of the U.S. manufacturers were into racing, automotive writers noted that American fabricators had to begin with a production car and beef up the engine and suspension to build a fast car. This over-stressed many components, especially the engines. They compared that to European manufacturers who began with a racing car and *detuned* it to build a fast car for street use. Obviously the latter approach under-stresses the engine and chassis. This was clearly seen on the early Ferrari GTs. We did our usual total restoration, but did not remove the body from the frame. This was one of the three cars I sold to Kirk White in December 1969.

Although Pinin Farina designed the body, Mario Boano constructed the first bodies, later known as the "Low Roof" Boanos. About a year later, Mario Boano sold his Carrozzeria Boano shop to his son-in-law, Ezio Ellena. The body design was changed a bit, with a higher roof and no vent windows. These have become known simply as the "High Roof" Boano. I bought a "High Roof" car, my second Boano, to restore in January 1975.

The 250 Colombo designed engines were still very similar to the 1953 250MM engines. The larger, dual point distributors were now mounted vertically at the rear of the engine, but the sparkplugs were still inside the V of the cam-covers. The oil filter was now one large permanent Fram-type, with changeable filter cartridge. The twin spin-on type was used soon thereafter on the Lusso Berlinettas. The generator was front-mounted, strapped to a cast aluminum saddle. The shaft extended through and out the front of the generator for a pulley that drove an aluminum fan blade mounted below. This fan placed too much load on the generator shaft bearings and was usually removed and replaced by an electric radiator fan. The fan may have been an expedient for driving the GT in traffic. Normally, the huge cooling capacity of the radiator and the aluminum pan designed to cool the oil kept the water temperature well in the normal range without the fan. After replacing the bearings in the generator, we left the fan off. The yellow Houdaille shock absorber could be seen below the exhaust header. This car was equipped with a heater, and for me, the hoses marred

Front and rear view of High Roof Boano, chassis no. 1285.

The Low Roof Boano bodied Ferrari GT, chassis no. 0785.

the aesthetics of the engine somewhat. I preferred cold feet and a neat engine compartment.

We trimmed the interior with high quality Bridge of Weir leather in the original seat pattern, but we pleated the door panels to match the diagonal slant of the doors. The original door panels were flat, with a gathered pocket. We also brought the carpet up about six inches on the door bottom to form a kick-panel. Also note that by this time, the Boano had left-hand steering.

This car was missing its front bumper and we were unable to find one before I sold it. These Italian bumpers, fabricated of very light gauge metal compared to the heavy bumpers on an American car of that era, rusted badly and would have been useless in a collision. We replaced all the rubber extrusions on these cars, some of which we had to have made. Loran's time cards showed that he had almost 1200 hours in this project, and of

Front and rear view of the Low Roof Boano.

The new leather interior (note left hand drive). The familiar 250 GT engine.

course that did not include the farmed-out engine machine work or the interior trim.

When I finished the last Boano, my cost was a little under $19,000. I sold it in 1979 to Dick Nordquist, a friend in the sign business in Minneapolis, Minnesota. Dick was sort of a Nordic giant, about 6' 4" tall. He loved sports cars but could not find one big enough for his long legs. He had seen and admired my Ferraris and I told him he should buy one because the GT cars were big enough for him to squeeze into, and maybe even drive. He had a 1967 Jaguar XK-E roadster that he had just completely restored but couldn't drive. I agreed to take it in trade for his cost and sell him the Ferrari at my cost. Since I still needed to break the engine in I agreed to drive the Ferrari to Minneapolis to swap cars.

I took the secondary highways up through Wyoming and South Dakota into Minnesota, and by the time I reached Minneapolis, the Ferrari engine was well broken in. While breaking it in I could not drive it really fast so the steering was heavy and the suspension was rather too firm. It was not a happy car at normal highway speed. With virtually no sound deadening it was also noisy in the passenger compartment. In short, it was tiring to drive on a long trip, regardless of what Ferrari intended them to be used for. By contrast, in spite of being a bit cramped for my frame of only six feet, the XK-E Jaguar was much smoother and quieter and was a thoroughly pleasant car to drive home at normal highway speed. Admittedly it was manufactured almost ten years after the Ferrari and it was a six-cylinder car. I also got $6,600 cash to boot. But I assured Dick that if he held onto the Ferrari he would make money on it. And he did both.

Dick didn't like the dark green paint color and repainted the car red in his own sign shop. I'm sure Dick Nordquist did OK when he sold it. It

I must admit I like it better in red, with our saddle interior.

was in the Matsuda collection in Japan from 1983 to 1995, when it came back to America.

Out of the blue in March 1997 I received a letter from Rick Marshall, who had purchased the car. He was pleased to get copies of my documentation and learn the details of the very comprehensive mechanical restoration we had done. The car was still red as Dick Nordquist had painted it and still had our leather interior when he got the car. Obviously, the car had been driven very little.

At best I about broke even on my cost for restoring these two Boano Ferraris. But at the time many of them were being dismantled for parts, and if nothing else, I saved two of the early cars from that probable fate. A restored Boano coupe is "only" worth about $200,000 today, and a rare aluminum bodied Boano recently sold for over $400,000. They will likely continue to rise in value as time goes by.

I must admit that I like the car better in red.

A good Boano Ferrari is valued at $300,000 today, and is considered an "entry-level" early Ferrari.

19

The Fire Alfa

If I had seen the picture below before I bought the remains I would never have tackled it. Fact is I did not see the picture until fifteen years after I had finished and sold the car. You see, it was like this. In a phone conversation my friend John O'Donnell, who always seemed to know where every Alfa in the country was, and whether or not any of them might be for sale, said a guy he knew had a genuine 6C-1750 Gran Sport Zagato

The photograph I saw only years after restoring this charred mess.

stored in his garage, and in John's words, "somebody torched it." (He was from New Jersey, after all.) He would never tell me the man's name, but he said the guy had been collecting parts for years and now had almost enough for a whole car. John thought he might be able to buy all this stuff. Naturally, I bit, and John set the hook.

This was in early 1979 and the supercharged Alfas were now bringing pretty big money. And it was highly unlikely that anyone in America was going to find a nice, whole old Alfa in somebody's chicken coop that the poor old widow just wanted someone to haul away, because it reminded her of her departed husband who bought it new. So I bought an incredible pile of parts from John for $12,000 FOB John's place. That's equivalent to $32,000 in current money. Admittedly, the parts were cleaned up by the time I got them. The fire, which had ruptured the gas tank on the Alfa, had virtually melted everything that was aluminum on the car. I got what was left of the original engine and two spare engines, two transmissions, a rear axle, a bunch of brake parts, plus all the steel parts of the burned car including the frame, springs, axles, firewall, wheels and many small parts from the original chassis #8513088.

While most of those steel parts could be rebuilt, they presented a formidable challenge that would test every specialty resource I knew of and would challenge Loran's talent as well. For my part it was knowing where I could get difficult things done and where I might find the things that were missing or unusable. The first thing was the steel frame, which was twisted and had lost its temper. It had to be straightened, then re-tempered. I made a drawing and translated the metric dimensions in Luigi Fusi's book to inches and decimal fractions, and we set up a jig. We first took it to a local collision repair shop just to straighten the frame. We attached diagonal cables and turnbuckles from corner to corner to hold it true, and Loran then strengthened it by welding continuous plates on the inside web for a major part of its length. We then sent it to another specialist in Denver where they put it in an oven to release the strains from all the welding, and then re-tempered the steel. We painted the frame and could now begin mounting components on the frame as we rebuilt or refinished them. The Alfas' firewalls were stamped from heavy-gauge steel, and were very strong. They contribute a great deal of strength to the light, flexible chassis frame. They are riveted to the frame and support the instrument panel, the wiring harness and fuse blocks as well as the cowl of the body. This one was undamaged by the fire. After a careful paint job Loran riveted it to the frame.

The wheels were warped and it would not be safe to rebuild them, but the heavy splined wheel hubs and those on the stub axles were good.

I sent the wheel hubs to England and ordered eighteen new wheels made, six for this car, six for the 6C-1750 Zagato which we were also now working on, and six spares to trade or sell.

The radiator was missing. I eventually traded a bunch of spare bits and pieces to Chris Mann in England for a used 1750 Alfa radiator, which we then had to repair, rebuild and dismantle to chrome plate the shroud. We had the front axle straightened and tempered.

The original Zagato body was completely destroyed in the fire, but the owner had found the rear bustle of what we believed to have been a Touring Alfa body, though there was no identification on it. John O'Donnell had provided the front fenders from another Alfa. We had to build the rest of the body, some of which we could do in our shop and some of which I would have done by others. It had taken about eighteen months to get this far along.

After having the three available engine blocks tested and magnafluxed, we chose engine # 10814402, which was originally a 1500cc racing engine. We took the best of everything from these three engines, magnafluxed all the critical parts and rebuilt the engine with the best of the crankshafts, rods, valves and valve guides. The exhaust headers of the original engine were OK, since they are made to withstand very high heat. We had only

Restoring and assembling parts, now in progress under wraps in the car shop.

one blower. From the headers back we had another stainless steel exhaust system made in England.

The biggest single problem we were confronted with was the lower cast aluminum intake manifold. This was a finned manifold that attached to one side of the blower with two right angle bends and bolted to the bottom of the six-port intake manifold that, in turn, bolted to the aluminum intake side of the head. Luckily for me, another genius came along. I didn't find Lee Gohlike; he found me. He was buying up all the old Mercedes and Alfa parts he could find. He was making replica parts for certain rare cars, especially the pre-war Mercedes. If I could provide casting patterns he agreed to make the missing manifold in trade for all the engine parts I was not going to use, which amounted to the better part of two engines. This was way over my head. Luigi Fusi at the Alfa Museum provided original drawings and specifications of the castings. I hired Tuck Jones to make the patterns for the castings. He was a draftsman recommended by the mechanics in Briggs Cunningham's museum in California. After sending Gohlike the patterns I called Lee regularly to check on the manifold. He kept promising it soon, but it was 10 months before we finally got it. By then, that was the last thing we needed to run the engine. The last I heard about Lee Gohlike he was building a replica Bucchiali from scratch. Only one real Bucchiali was ever built, and there was some doubt that it ever ran.

We sent the springs to Phil Reilly to be arched and rebuilt. He had a good source for such work and was willing to help. Loran, meanwhile, had made wood patterns and the bronze castings for the fold-down windshield, the radiator cap and other small parts. A metal casting shrinks as it cools, by a known percentage. We had to estimate the shrinkage, and make the wood patterns that much larger for the finished parts to be the same as the original parts. Loran surprised me by making the fabricated

The finished engine, built with the best parts from three engines.

The finished car—a small miracle!

chrome plated body trim. I had been worrying about how we could do it. I assumed the only way Loran could do it was to saw ⅛" thick sheet aluminum to shape, then file and polish it. Loran made wood patterns for the left and right sides, then made the parts from soft thin brass sheet, which he peened to shape with a light hammer. It formed nicely over the wood patterns and work-hardened the metal at the same time so that it was no longer soft. This was the same way the Italians had made it and it looked great on the car when it was finished. Loran was at his best doing things like this.

From Bosch in Germany I had found a source that still stocked new old-style Bosch headlights. These were not identical to the original Bosch that was used on the Alfas, but they were the immediately following generation and still fit the stanchions without any changes. Loran made the taillights. Loran also made up all new wiring for the car. I sent what instruments we got with the car to John Marks in England for rebuilding, and he provided those instruments we were lacking. I had a new radiator stone guard made. Loran made a new gas tank of lead-plated tern-metal that would never rust. We could not get the delicate float parts to work inside the firewall mounted fuel vacuum tank, so we installed a hidden electric pump near the gas tank, and piped it through the vacuum tank so that it looked original.

Loran built new seat frames with new seat springs, and we had the leather trim work done locally. Phil Reilly rebuilt the multiple plate clutch

A very handsome Alfa. Chassis no. 8513088, engine no. 10814402.

I wish I had it back to drive again in Estes Park!

assembly. We ordered new reproduction badges and chassis number plates from W.C. Williams. The car was first started and running in October of 1984, almost five years after we began. But the results were good, considering what we started with.

One can only imagine how proud both Loran and I were of this project. It was pure madness to have taken it on, but this car, probably more than any car we ever did, tells where my real interests were—in the actual rebuilding of the cars!

By 1983 I had been in the electric sign industry for almost forty years. I had been relatively successful, and I derived a pretty broad business education from the sign industry because our clientele were exclusively owners of businesses big and small and of every type. It was time I retired, at least partially. We moved to Estes Park, Colorado, a beautiful small town in the mountains at an altitude of 7,500 feet. It was a town of about 6,000 permanent residents, but because it was the gateway to Rocky Mountain National Park, about three million people went through town in the summer season. We built a new home there in 1984. That year I had to have some rather serious surgery and I reasoned that I should stop risking the considerable amount of money that my car hobby now represented. If something should happen to me I didn't want to leave several unfinished cars for Jackie and our son to deal with and dispose of. At that particular time, I had the Fire Alfa, the 6C-1750 Zagato that was nearly finished, an 8C-2.3 Alfa that is the subject of my next chapter and one of my Talbot Lagos that was finished but not yet sold. These cars had an aggregate value of about $500,000 at the time.

I had Loran bring the Fire Alfa up to my new home in Estes Park, where I could drive it to break the engine in properly and be sure everything was OK. This car was what the British call a Bittsa. A bitsa-this and a bitsa that. For that reason it would never be a truly valuable Alfa. That didn't mean it was any less fun to drive or less beautiful to see.

I was never happy with the recess in the body for the two spare tires. It was too large in diameter for the 1750 tires, which made me believe this body may have been for a 2.3 Alfa that had larger wheels. I drove the car in the mountains to break the engine in. I liked to take the car up Highway 7, south of Estes to Allenspark, which was about 9,000 feet elevation. The supercharger compensates to some extent for the effect of altitude because it compresses the air/gas mixture. The Alfa ran great, even at that altitude, and in fact was quite fast. We had done a good job of rebuilding the steering, the springs and shocks, and I was pleased with the way it handled. I put about four hundred miles on the car, but while making my favorite run, I heard a ticking noise that I feared was a rod bearing. I sent the car back to Loran in my van. He had to pull the engine again, and on close examination we found that the rod bolts had stretched when they were torqued to the proper specification. We found some new Ford rod bolts that could be used, and after re-babbitting three of the rods and boring them to fit the shaft properly, Loran reinstalled the engine and I drove it another couple hundred miles. I advertised the car in *Hemmings*, and following a full disclosure of just what the car was, and what we had done to it, I sold the car to Dan Margulies, a dealer in London, for $75,000, equal to about $140,000 in today's money. It probably isn't worth much more than that now, because of its pieced-together nature. An all-original Alfa like this one would be worth three or four times as much now. In spite of the difficulty of this project I made a small profit and Dan Margulies wrote to tell me he was very pleased with the car.

I lost track of the car for several years until I noticed it was to be auctioned by Christie's in Monaco. It returned to the U.S. and while Don Young owned it he had Phil Reilly & Co. rebuild the engine again. It was in 1999 when Ivan Zaremba of Reilly & Co. sent me the photo of the car when it was destroyed by fire, with a note congratulating me for having saved another Alfa. That was the first time I had seen the photo.

I wish I had it back, to drive again in Estes Park!

Even as a "Bitsa" this Alfa is worth $150,000 in today's market.

20

My Last
8C-2.3 Alfa Romeo

This Alfa was first sold in 1933 to the Montecatini Company for 70,000 lire ($4,700 U.S.). It was a long chassis, clothed in a very pretty cabriolet body, probably by Farina. It went to Guy Neville Montagu in England in 1948. Its history is unknown until the early '60s, when it was owned by William White, who lived in the country northwest of Chicago. Keith Hellon believes the lady in the picture is Mrs. White.

Keith Hellon met Mr. White in the mid–1960s when he asked Keith to shorten the chassis to have a replica Zagato Spider body built by Jack Henser at Proto Products in a suburb of Detroit. Keith says the original body was beyond salvaging. The shortened chassis was completed in about 1970 and was sent to Proto Products. When a dispute arose between White and Henser over billing, the work was stopped and the project languished for ten years! Bill White and Jack Henser were no longer even speaking. Mr. White had the dismantled engine and drivetrain at his home, and Jack Henser had the chassis, including the firewall, cowl and radiator, in Detroit.

I had continued my search for another 8C-2.3 Alfa to restore and this time, I was determined to keep it for myself. Keith told me about this car of White's, but he doubted that it could be acquired. Several people had tried to buy it, but White was known as a difficult person. Moreover, after building most of the replica aluminum body, Jack Henser was holding it and the chassis against money due him. Keith thought that Henser may even have sold his part of the car to get his money.

With trepidation, I called Mr. White and asked him if he would sell

The original Farina cabriolet body.

the car. He said yes, but that several people had "wanted to steal it." He said I could make just one offer. If the offer were too low, he would not haggle. He refused to tell me a price he would take for the car. I discussed the problem of his dispute with Jack Henser and he agreed that if my offer was fair and acceptable, he would settle with Henser. I could see why some people might think he was difficult. I asked him to call Jack Henser to be sure he would settle the dispute with Mr. White and release the parts that he had to me.

I gave this some serious thought, estimated what I expected the restoration would cost, and concluded the most I should offer was $18,000. I called Mr. White with my offer and he said he thought it was a fair price. He was much easier to deal with thereafter. I had not met him in person but now went to his home to verify and inventory everything he had, and to request an inventory of what Henser had. I wanted to be sure it was the whole basic car and the aluminum body. We got along fine when I met him at his home. We were both businessmen, although he had been retired for a long time. He told me that his family had been in the bottling business and had invented and patented the crimp-type bottle cap. I had a couple of patents too, but mine pertained to relatively unimportant aluminum extrusion sign frame systems. I thought of all the products that were sold in bottles with a crimped cap, and I could see why it had supported the White family for a long time.

Their home was not ostentatious, but a nice country home. Bill had

The Alfa when it was brought to the U.S. from England. Keith Hellon believes the woman is Mrs. White, wife of William White.

the dismantled engine in his basement and the rest of the parts, other than what Henser had, in the loft of his barn. We spent half a day inventorying everything, and the only missing part was the external oil gallery line for the engine. He thought it was around somewhere, but we never found it. I paid Bill White and he paid Henser, who was glad, after ten years, to finally get his money.

I sent Loran with my truck to pick up the parts, and then on to Detroit to get everything Henser had. When Loran returned, we began the restoration in 1980 and completed it in 1983. I made a full-size side elevation drawing of the Zagato body, using the illustrations in Luigi Fusi's book. I had seen a number of replica bodied Alfas that were all out of proportion. This is where my designer's eye and drafting skill helped a lot.

We mounted the raw aluminum body on the car, and I could see that the front fenders were too tall, too long and out of proportion. Henser had not finished the body completely. The running boards, rear fenders and twin battery boxes were not yet made. I offered to pay Henser's airfare, room and food expenses to come to Fort Collins to correct the fenders. I had bought an old wheeling machine for Loran, but he never used it. Henser came and worked about a week correcting the fenders. I got the impression he had fallen on rather hard times, and that he was in poor

The engine and transmission finished, assembly progresses.

Body completed and fitted; it will come apart to be painted in pieces.

Suspension and brakes completed, new floorboards and aluminum battery boxes made.

Loran first test-drives the car in our back lot.

health. I had the running boards built in Los Angeles, and the rear fenders and battery boxes built in Atlanta by a young Englishman that had recently moved to the U.S.

We rebuilt and restored the chassis and engine first. The body was fitted in sections and each section was then removed and painted off the chassis before the final assembly: the axles, brakes, engine, steering, transmission, and (black) dry-sump oil tank under the frame and firewall.

The wheels, aluminum and wood floor pans were next. The aluminum battery and toolboxes were mounted over the rear axle. The accompanying pictures will be of interest to anyone restoring a 6C or 8C Alfa. The polished brake drums and backer-plates and the highly detailed engine components are "over-restored," but that was beginning to be what it took for winning at Concours d' Élégance events in the U.S. at that time. Some European restoration shops were beginning to restore them to look like a very well maintained original car with a patina. While I had no intention of showing this car, we admittedly were guilty of lily-gilding too. We resisted chrome plating the wheels, however.

About two years had gone by since we began this project. Loran was working on three cars at the same time, however. He had to make all the castings for the fold-down windshield, and also made the Zagato style body trim from thin sheet-brass, peened to shape over hardwood forms, then filed smooth, then chrome plated.

All the body panels in primer are fitted and adjusted as necessary

One of the most beautiful automobile engines ever built.

The oil tank was on the passenger side, with the filler cap through the running board. Brakes adjust with knurled knob at top.

before any finished painting begins. They are then dismantled and the principal parts, such as the fenders, cowl, doors, bustle and hood panels, are each painted separately. We placed two inch wide felt between the body and the frame, and black welting was used between the fenders, body and running boards to prevent squeaking.

The cockpit was pretty comfortable. Note the gated shift tower, with lockout tab for reverse, and the pedal arrangement.

The perfectly proportioned Zagato replica body on the completely restored chassis.

Loran got the first drive in our back parking lot on a cold winter day. Then I drove it for a while. When the hood was lifted the eight-branch exhaust with stainless pipes and the aluminum eight-branch intake manifold and blower sparkled in the sun like jewelry. There is no doubt in my mind that these were among the most beautiful engines in the world.

We sent the car out for the leather upholstering and gray Wilton wool carpets. Padded leather trim covered the cowl and door tops. A blue dial below the instrument panel was for adjusting the Siata friction shock absorbers by sheathed wires to each one, for a firm or softer ride.

I had the car finished to please myself because I intended to keep this Alfa. I was very pleased with the results of about 2,000 man-hours of work, mostly by Loran, spread over almost three years' time. I was especially pleased with the perfect proportions of the replica Zagato body that even carried replica Zagato body badges on the lower door panels. The radiator with Monza grill, wire mesh stone-guard, headlights, hood-latches, radiator badges and dumb-iron apron were all original parts. I was pleased with every aspect of the car.

The polished aluminum brake drums and backer plates with our signature gray-painted suspension parts made a beautiful contrast. A vertical thumbscrew above the kingpin permitted adjustment of the brake shoes without removing a wheel—another feature indicative of a racing design heritage.

I thought it was one of the best restorations we had ever done. Even though my Alfa had a replica body and the chassis was shortened, it was all Alfa and I didn't care. A totally original short-chassis Zagato was worth about $250,000 by then, but I had no idea how much the prices would soon skyrocket!

Even though I wanted to keep this car, it didn't work out that way. As told in the 6C-1750 Zagato chapter, to satisfy Tom Perkins, I sold him this car and took the 6C-1750 back. The 8C 2.3 Alfa stayed in his collection until the late 1980s when it was sold to Chris Mann in England. It passed through the hands of Brian Classic and the Christie's auction in Monaco in 1990. I last knew of it when owned by Carl Bloechle in Zurich.

The current Sports Car Market Price Guide *value of this Alfa is $1,500,000.*

21

An Idyllic Interlude

In 1981 a number of events converged to change my life. Some inventions I patented for building electric signs became important enough that my company turned from building custom electric signs for regional businesses to the wholesale side of the sign industry. With money made available by selling two of my cars, I bought five acres fronting on Interstate 25 in Fort Collins and built a new 32,000 square foot facility. From there, to this day, the company sells products and services at wholesale to the electric sign industry nationwide.

I leased my former plant on College Avenue, which is the main street in Fort Collins, to another sign company with the provision that I would keep the car shop there until Loran finished the three cars he was working on at the time, one of which was the 8C-2.3 with the replica Zagato body. When he finished that in 1983, Loran opened his own restoration shop. To help him get started he suggested restoring cars for me at a reasonable hourly rate plus his overhead cost if I would continue providing at least one car at a time.

By 1983 I had been an independent businessman for over forty years. I decided to semi-retire, but I still wanted to be somewhat engaged in our business. I turned the company management over to my son and my nephew, Gordon Brooks, both of whom had worked for the company for many years. Jackie and I moved to Estes Park.

The types of cars that interested me had become too valuable for a hobby. The last three cars that Loran worked on amounted to an aggregate investment of about $350,000. For me, that was no longer hobby money— it was becoming a business and I didn't need or want another business. I felt that I needed to make a clean break with my car hobby. Having sold the last of my cars by 1985, I tried to forget them. I gave most of my tools to Loran. I even sold most of my car books and what few Alfa and Ferrari parts I had. We became socially active in Estes Park. That came naturally for Jackie but it was a first for me. We met a lot of wonderful people and made many good friends. I also designed and built two homes in Estes.

But like a childhood sweetheart, I could never fully get cars out of my mind. Thinking an old car might be fun to have in Estes, I bought a 1932 Packard Model 902 phaeton in 1987. It had an older restoration and was a former CCCA 1st Senior car. I had read about Packards, the undisputed best selling pre-war luxury car in the world. They sold more cars than all other luxury makes combined, including Rolls-Royce and Cadillac. They were especially known for the quality of their engines and fine craftsmanship, and many Packards had custom bodies built by America's finest coachbuilders. My first Packard had a factory-built body, with green leather. We drove it for pleasure, took friends for picnics in Rocky Mountain National Park, just a few miles from our house in Estes, and drove it in holiday parades. I paid $65,000 for the Packard, and never did anything to it except drive it occasionally for pure pleasure.

As usual, I wanted to learn more about Packard, and bought a couple of books: Robert Turnquist's *Packard* and Beverly Rae Kimes' definitive book, *Packard: A History of the Car and the Company*. I was never particularly interested in American cars of the Classic era—defined by the Classic Car Club of America (CCCA) as encompassing certain specific fine cars manufactured from 1925 to World War II. Naturally, I joined the CCCA to get their very nice monthly bulletins and quarterly magazine. I soon discovered that it was a club primarily dominated by Packard owners and secondarily by Cadillac owners. Only those automobiles that were approved by CCCA could participate in club events as Classic Cars. Dozens of makes, including most of those I had ever owned, were approved by CCCA, but while these and many other makes were appreciated and welcomed by the members, they were vastly outnumbered by Packards and Cadillacs.

I was never much of a club joiner, nor had I been interested in showing cars to win awards in competition. I soon found that it usually required a 100-point car to win first in class at the national CCCA meets. The winners were frequently "trailer queens" that were seldom, if ever, driven on the road. They didn't necessarily even have to drive, for when judged, they merely had to be started and the engine run without moving the car. It didn't matter whether or not the engine and the rest of the mechanical parts of the car had been restored, although they almost always were. As long as the car was cosmetically perfect it could win. Absolutely correct and

The 1932 Packard Model 902 Phaeton, with grandkids Tyler and Jordyn Brooks.

The perfect picnic and parade car. Note the aftermarket fold-down rear windshield.

authentic parts were essential even if most of those parts could come from different cars of the same make and model. It had to have the correct nuts and bolts, engine and firewall labels and engine enamel color before it could win. The upholstery, bodywork, paint, chrome, tires and accessories had to be perfect, of the correct type and period. A 100-point car was always gorgeous and achieving that 100-point award added a lot of cash value to the car.

National CCCA meetings are held in several regions simultaneously. When a car takes first place in its class at any national CCCA meet, it receives a small body badge indicating it was a "First Junior." If it wins again, at another CCCA National meet, another piece is added to the badge reading "First Senior." After winning a third time, the car is badged as a senior premier and retired from competition and the owner can then enjoy the car by driving it without worrying about getting a nick in the paint. Many owners will then sell the car, advertised as a CCCA First Senior car, get top price for it, buy another car to restore and do it all over again. Others collect cars. The badge stays with the car permanently to prove it was once a Senior CCCA winner. This was not the sort of thing I restored cars for, although a few of my cars, after I sold them, won prizes at Pebble Beach, the most prestigious Concours d'Élégance of them all. I restored my cars to drive!

Even though I was invited I never attended any CCCA meetings in Denver and never took this Packard to any meets or shows. Zach Brinker-hoff, from Denver, was an avid CCCA member and a collector, especially of Packard automobiles. He and a friend came to Estes Park to see my car. He had a Packard of the same year, model and type awaiting restoration. We had a nice ride in my Packard. Several years later I learned that Zach Brinkerhoff was a very wealthy oilman, but I found him to be a very nice, down-to-earth man when it came to talking Classic cars. That's one of the nice things about this hobby.

My Packard's fifteen-year-old restoration was getting pretty tired cosmetically. It was beginning to need repainting and some chrome plating, but to do this work correctly would be a major project of dismantling much of the car. I decided to let the next owner make that decision. I sold it through a broker and made a $30,000 profit from it—another case of having my cake and eating it too.

In reading about Classic cars, I had become quite impressed by Pierce Arrow automobiles and the company that had built them. Like almost all of the American Classics, Pierce Arrow became a victim of the Depression. Most American automobiles were manufactured in Detroit, but Pierce Arrows were made in Buffalo, New York. The company began as a manufacturer of birdcages and bicycles. When they began making cars shortly after the turn of the century, the Pierce Arrow Company was blessed with some of the finest engineers in the industry and directors committed to building their cars to the highest possible quality standards. They were also

The 1932 eight-cylinder Pierce Arrow Club Brougham.

extremely conservative and were even more expensive than Packards. Their sales numbers were but a fraction of Packard's.

My Packard was a straight-eight cylinder model and one of the lowest priced for their 1932 line. When I saw an equivalent 1932 Pierce Arrow Club Brougham for sale I bought it for $37,000. It was a very nice amateur restoration, mostly done by the owner, but with a professional paint job.

Two factors accounted for difference in value between the Packard and the Pierce. First, the Pierce was a closed car and the Packard was a convertible. Second, for a comparable car a Pierce was only worth about two-thirds as much as a Packard at the time I bought it. This Pierce had a known history from its beginning, having always been in California. I don't believe it left the factory with the paint colors it had when I got it, but as a whole, the car was very nice and it had the advantage of being an all-weather car. We do get winter in Colorado.

The engines of the Packard and the Pierce were so smooth and quiet you could hardly hear them idling. Without question both were fine cars for their era. The main and rod bearings of the engines at that time had poured babbitt, not at all comparable to modern insert bearing shells. And

Note the bypass oil filter we added to the engine.

amazingly, neither car had an oil filter, as we now know them. The first thing I did to both cars was to drill and tap a line from the internal oil gallery to fit a canister type bypass filter. This was not a full-flow filter that pumps all the oil through the filter. A bypass only pumps a small part of the oil, but over time, it still helps to remove carbon. We may chuckle at the crudity of these old cars today, but in 1932, a new Ford sold for about $450, and a Packard or Pierce Arrow cost at least six or seven times as much! I kept the Pierce for several years and I believe it was actually a better quality car, but I liked the looks of the Packard better as did everyone else in my family. It was a convertible and it was just more fun! Everyone who saw the Packard smiled.

During our ten years in Estes Park, in addition to our ordinary transportation cars, I had two more cars that were very special. When Gene Rouse and I first began buying Mercedes for our family cars in 1965, Daimler Benz was building a super-luxury, cost-no-object car to rebuild their image as one of the world's finest automobiles. World War II had destroyed their factories and their image as well. There was a lot of resistance among wealthy Americans, especially Jews, towards buying a Mercedes automobile. A Jewish friend in Denver once made the macabre joke that he would love to have a 280 SL but he was afraid he might find his uncle in the upholstering! This new, very special ultra-luxury car was produced in small numbers from 1964 through 1972 for the U.S. and international markets. It was made in two wheelbase lengths: the SWB owner-driver limousine and the Pullman. The latter was huge, with six doors, and was sold to heads of state, the Pope, dictators and the extremely wealthy Eastern potentates. The one Gene and I would have liked to own was the short wheelbase model. But they sold for $12,000 in 1964 ($75,000 in today's money), so we forgot that! Just reading about them made us drool. They had a six-liter V-8 engine that produced 300 hp and over 300 ft lbs. of torque. They weighed almost 6,000 pounds, yet were the fastest luxury sedans in the world at that time. They were hand-built in Mercedes' Sindelfingen Factory with the very finest wood and leather interiors and the very latest technology. All the power features, such as the locks, windows and seat adjustments, were hydraulically controlled. When only partially closed the doors would then silently close tightly by hydraulic fingers. There was front and rear air conditioning of course, with a refrigerated compartment under the front armrest that contained four small crystal wine glasses and a thermos. The back armrest console opened with a cosmetic vanity and nail-care set. Even the back seats were hydraulically controlled for fore and aft adjustment. In terms of comfort features those cars were the forerunners of the latest modern S-Class Mercedes.

I had read about them from time to time and when a very good 1969 model turned up for sale in Portland, Oregon, I bought it for $65,000 and picked it up on our next trip to visit Jackie's parents in Chinook, Washington. We drove it the long way home through Montana and Yellowstone. Even in 1990, when the car was already twenty-one years old, you knew you were driving something very special.

While I was driving about 100 mph in Montana, a patrolman's lights

The 1969 600 Mercedes. What an automobile!

appeared in my rear-view window. Montana had a prima facie speed limit then, meaning no set speed, but a speed that was considered safe. Nevada had the same speed law then. When this policeman came up to the car, he said we were going a little over 100. I mentioned that there was very little traffic, and that we were just enjoying driving their great rolling hill country. He suggested we hold it down a bit, then he asked about the car. He said he had never seen one like it. I got out, opened the hood and told him about the car. He was impressed and left us by saying "have a nice day"—and we did.

Now, *that* was an automobile. I have been tempted several times to buy another 600 SWB, but if I wait awhile, and remember how much it cost to replace the combination water and oil pump, the urge goes away. We drove the 600 Mercedes on a couple of vacations, and I drove it quite a bit up and down the Big Thompson canyon to our company offices in Fort Collins. I broke even when I sold it. It was not a great mountain car, it was just too big and heavy for a twisting, curving mountain highway, but on an interstate highway—let the good times roll!

The other unusual car I had in Estes Park was a 1972 Citroën SM. The "SM" stands for Sports-Maserati. John (Matt) Mattingly, who invented the Water-Pic, was a friend and neighbor. Phyllis, his wife, was fluent in French and they drove a Citroën sedan that they loved. By 1970, when the Citroën SM came on the market in the U.S., Matt had become pretty affluent and bought a new SM. Since I was his only friend who appreciated cars, he brought his brand-new SM to my plant to have me see and drive it. First, he opened the hood to reveal an engine compartment like I had never seen before. The double-overhead cam Maserati V-6 engine was only about 12" long. It was turned backwards and mounted far back with a shaft coming forward that drove all the auxiliary equipment, of which there was a plethora!

Before I drove the car Matt warned that the steering was *very* quick— with only a three-quarter turn lock-to-lock! And it was progressively hydraulically assisted, with decreasing assist as speed increased. It had a built-in self-centering of the steering. You could crank the wheels, turn off the engine and the wheels would center themselves! People who parked on a hill and made a practice of turning the wheels into the curb to prevent the car from rolling down the hill had to turn off the engine then press the brakes repeatedly to dissipate the accumulator's carry-over hydraulic power to the steering. Matt also warned me about the brakes. They are big four-wheel discs, also hydraulically assisted, operated by a ball on the floor where a pedal is located on other cars! Matt said to test it gingerly, because the brakes were *very* powerful. And they were!

The 1972 Citroën SM. The M indicates the Maserati engine.

In fact, everything about the car was hydraulically controlled. Next to the driver's seat, near the floor, was a lever with three settings to adjust the car's height from the ground. The highest was to change a tire without a jack! When the car's ignition was turned off, the steering centered itself, then with a sigh the car settled very low to the ground. When the engine was started, it rose like a camel, first the rear end, then the front, to the normal driving position. I remember reading what some wag said: "Citroën is not a car factory—it's a laboratory!" There is no question but what the French indeed do march to a different drummer when it comes to cars—and just about everything else, too, come to think of it.

John Mattingly was a mechanical engineer, just the sort of person that could appreciate the Citroën SM. They were expensive too. John paid well over $11,000 for it from the Denver dealer. By comparison a new Ferrari cost about $13,000 at that time. I drove John's car only once, but I never forgot the experience. When I had an opportunity to buy a very fine SM in 1991 from a doctor in Las Vegas for about what they had cost new, I just had to own one, at least for a while. The doctor was the second owner. The original owner in Los Angeles had the dealer do some additional cosmetic polishing and detailing to the engine compartment, so it was even more dramatic when you opened the hood.

The engine compartment layout was very different from most cars.

The SM designers tested it in a wind tunnel to minimize wind resistance. It had the lowest coefficient of drag of any production car in the world at that time, something on the order of .023 as I recall. Some considered the SM to be one of the best looking cars of the 21st century, while others thought it was the ugliest car in the world. Beauty is indeed in the eyes of the beholder, and is also very subjective. My opinion was somewhere in-between.

The front end of the European model had tempered glass covering the four headlamps, a pair of which turned with the steering. Those were illegal in the U.S., although they can be found. The rear end was the least attractive in my opinion, possibly because of its airfoil design. The overall build quality was very good and excellent quality materials were used for the interior. The buyer had a choice of a good five-speed manual transmission or a truly awful Borg Warner automatic. By all means, one should opt for the manual! The manual transmission also increases the car's resale value considerably in today's (very limited) market. In my opinion, these cars are possibly the most under-rated and under-valued collectable cars in the U.S. They have been praised by some car magazines and denigrated by others. I wonder if their detractors have ever really driven one. That's

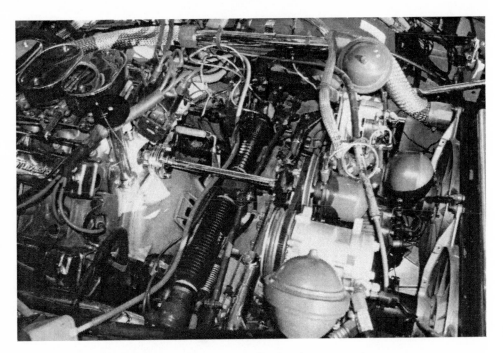

The SM was a masterpiece of hydraulic engineering.

not to say they were perfect. The V-6 Maserati engine was quickly adapted for the SM by eliminating two cylinders from their V-8 engine. This resulted in a slight imbalance that was only partially eliminated by twin chains turning the camshafts in opposite directions in the opposing banks of cylinders. The 3-liter engine produced 170 horsepower, enabling a top speed of 135 mph. Admittedly they are different, and it takes a few hours behind the wheel to become completely adjusted to the very fast steering, but when one does, one may wonder why all cars were not like the SM! It was always a fun car to drive. Its decline in popularity was made worse by Citroën's withdrawal from the U.S. shortly after production ceased on the SM. I have found, though, that parts for almost any foreign car ever sold in the U.S. are available somewhere, somehow, by someone.

Looking under the hood can be frightening at first, seeing all the stuff not found on an ordinary car. The engine sat far back, with three Weber carburetors. Two outside green spheres were for the front suspension (there were two more for the rear), and in the center was the hydraulic accumulator, a reserve pressure sphere that provided power after the engine was turned off. The original owner had fitted a polished aluminum hood liner to reflect the glorious engine compartment when he was showing the car.

I used my SM for everyday transportation for a couple of years, going up and down the Big Thompson River canyon to Fort Collins three times a week. It was always a fun drive, especially in the mountains, and it was always a reliable, comfortable car, regardless of the weather conditions.

With front-wheel drive, the clutch and transmission were in front of the engine, below all the auxiliary equipment. The big front disc brakes were mounted inboard. The hydraulically controlled rack and pinion steering was just above the transmission. The high-pressure hydraulic pump, alternator and air conditioning equipment were all driven off the crankshaft by the chrome-plated shaft in the center. There were twin, thermostatically controlled, electric radiator cooling fans. This car was a mechanical tour de force!

The Citroën SM had the most comfortable ride of any car I have ever driven, smoothing out even the roughest railroad tracks. The shock-absorbing spheres had a diaphragm with compressible nitrogen gas, I recall, above the diaphragm. The spheres simply unscrewed for easy service; one sent them to a service center (which still exists) for exchange and screwed the replacements on. John Mattingly bought an old country estate north of Fort Collins, with some rather rough terrain, on which he built a commercial glider-port. Rather than going the long way around by the road to the glider port, he raised the SM to the middle setting from the ground and took the shortcut over his ditches and fields. He loved that car and kept it for many years.

One complaint I had of the SM was that in spite of the complex and expensive factory exhaust system the engine drone became tiring on a long trip. Very good Citroën SMs can be had for $15,000 to $20,000 at this time. They are easy to work on for those who are mechanically inclined, and they are a real bargain! English-language shop manuals are available, and a good amateur mechanic can do most of the routine maintenance work.

Michelin owned Citroën at the time the SM was built, and a bit later they also acquired Maserati. This led to the Maserati Bora being built with many of the SM's hydraulic features. While not as all encompassing as they are on the SM, these hydraulic systems have nevertheless made the Bora a much less sought-after collectable than it would have been without them. I thought about buying a Bora more than once, but after a good night's sleep, the urge went away.

The ten years we spent in Estes Park were the best years of our lives. We were still young enough to do most anything we wanted, and I stopped working enough to enjoy those years. But by 1993 I was 71 years old, approaching the normal life span of 73 years for American males. In 1991 I was profoundly brought face-to-face with my mortality when, in the span of four months, my mother and both of my brothers died. I was the last survivor in my personal family. My mother lived in good health to the age of 95 but my brothers both died of esophageal cancer. Jackie and I were developing some arthritis and the altitude and steep mountainous terrain were making it difficult for us to walk as much as we should. We decided to move back to Fort Collins at only 5,000 feet elevation, where the terrain was flat, where our family and business were, where our doctors and dentists were, and where there was much more accessible medical care if we should need it.

We scouted the valley for a home, but finding nothing we liked, I designed and built a new home, with a four-car garage, on 2.5 acres in the country, near Windsor, about ten miles from Fort Collins. There were even more paved country roads with very little traffic on which I could drive my cars through the beautiful countryside with a full view of the high Rocky Mountains to the west.

22

The Nash Healy

From everything I have read, had there not been an accidental meeting of two men aboard a ship headed from England to New York, there would never have been a Nash Healy. Beginning with a discussion about cameras, they discovered a mutual interest in automobiles. These two very different gentlemen were from totally different ends of the automobile industry. The version I read indicated that Donald Healy was on his way to Detroit to try to coax Cadillac engines out of General Motors to use in a new sports-racing chassis he had in mind. The other gentleman was George Mason, president of Nash Kelvinator, soon to become American Motors, through a merger with the fast fading Hudson Motor Company. When Mason learned of Donald Healy's mission, he invited him to be his house guest while he was in Detroit, and when Healy was not successful with Cadillac, Mason suggested using the Nash Ambassador engine and running gear. George Mason had already made a deal with Pinin Farina to work with his designers to breathe new life into the Nash line of automobiles. He thought that building a high performance sports car that bore the Nash name would increase both interest and sales. So it came to pass that between Donald Healy and George Mason a totally impractical agreement was made. It was to build an "American" sports car by shipping the engine, transmission and brakes from America to Donald Healy, who would install his steering and "trailing link" front suspension system and work his magic on the engine to increase its power. He would build the aluminum body, then ship it to America to be sold as an American car!

But first came the racing to gain fame and publicity. Mason provided the Nash Ambassador's six-cylinder pushrod engine with a hotter cam. It already had a seven main bearing crankshaft, and Donald Healy designed a new aluminum head with two 1¾" side-draft S.U. carburetors that boosted the power to 125 bhp. It had a three-speed transmission with a fourth gear as an electric overdrive. The first cars sported an all aluminum body built by Panel Craft. It was now ready for racing, at which Donald Healy was no slouch. He had been an R.A.F. pilot in the First World War after which he began constructing and racing his own fast cars, the last of which were the Silverstone Healys. He entered the Nash Healy in the 1950 24 Hours of Le Mans in France, and gave Europe's best cars a bad time, winning fourth overall in 1950 and sixth overall in 1951. He took first in class and third overall in 1952. Fifty-eight cars started but only seventeen finished! This proved beyond all doubt that the Nash Healy engine was extremely strong and reliable. Meanwhile, 104 cars with the English body, leather upholstery, and an adjustable steering wheel were built in this period and shipped to America. All this shipping back and forth made for a very high price. Then, to complicate matters further, George Mason wanted a new Pinin Farina body for the Nash Healy, so the chassis was first shipped to England, the Healy modified running chassis was then shipped to Italy, and finally the finished car was shipped to America for sale! For 1954 Farina built only long-wheelbase hardtop coupes, called the Le Mans. Even at a very high price that resulted in few sales, the Nash Healy was a money loser for American Motors. Then, when George Mason died suddenly, George Romney became the new president of American Motors and pulled the plug on the Nash Healy. Only 402 Farina-built bodies were built, and a grand total of 506 Nash Healys were built from December 1950 through August of 1954. They were rare by any standard.

I had admired the Pinin Farina bodied Nash Healy for some time, but it was never taken seriously as a real sports car in America in spite of its performance at Le Mans. They didn't turn up for sale very often, and when they did they were usually basket cases. I found that a gentleman in Pennsylvania was trying to corner the market on Nash Healys. He had a whole barn full of them, but wouldn't consider selling one of his. However, he told me an interesting story, and sent me the written copy to back it up.

After the Nash Healy went out of production, American Motors produced a state of the art V-8 high performance engine for its Ambassador, and a couple of the company's engineers began to ponder what a different story the Nash Healy might have had had it been given this new engine. The two engineers and an art director had Healy roadsters, and to find out, they stuffed this V-8 engine into two of the cars. After doing so, the engineers wrote a paper telling exactly how anyone that wanted to do this "semi-factory" modification could do it properly. They gave the part numbers for the engine mounts and other factory parts needed, and only a small cut and weld had to be done to one side of the frame to clear the starter.

When Loran first opened his own car shop I bought a 1953 Nash Healy roadster that was in poor but running condition. I drove it enough to determine what all it might need. The rear end was quiet and the transmission was good, but the electric overdrive wasn't working and some of the instruments were not working. The painted instrument panel needed repainting and the chrome plating was bad. The top irons needed replating, too, and that meant totally dismantling them. This required drilling out the special rivets and machining new ones when the top irons came back from the plater. The engine needed an overhaul, so I decided to find one of the 327 cubic inch Nash Ambasador engines to rebuild and put in the Nash Healy. The car had to be pretty well taken apart to do all the painting, plating, cosmetic and mechanical work. I found a 1957 Ambassador engine at a local wrecking yard. We did a routine rebuild of this engine for which parts were not a problem. Loran repainted the engine compartment before the engine went in. He also stripped and refinished the instrument panel and we had the instruments that were not working repaired. A rather major undertaking was rewiring the car from six volts to twelve volts in preparation for the later engine installation. Loran repaired the electric overdrive switches and we had to use a 12 to 6 volt converter for the instruments that still operated by six volts.

When the engine was finished he installed it following the factory engineer's printed manual. We ordered the parts required from an AMC parts source, by part number. Loran cut the notch out of the frame flange and reinforced it according to the instruction, and we were ready to shoehorn the engine in. It was a tight fit getting it in, and as I recall, it had to be lifted up from under the car. Loran had stripped the car to bare metal and repainted it in a Mercedes color I had chosen. I tried to clean up the wire wheels that came with the car but found them too far gone. I bought five aftermarket wire wheels of the same size, with the same spoke pattern as used by the factory. These had generic hubcaps, with no name on them, so I masked them with latex, cut the stencils and sprayed the Nash Healy script on them. A new set of radial tires finished the basic car. The car still had good vinyl seats but I had them re-upholstered in red leather and had red carpets and a new black cloth top made. It turned out very well.

But the real surprise came when I first drove the car. It was a lot like my experience had been when I put the Lusso Berlinetta Ferrari engine in the little type 166 Ferrari Roadster. The original 166 Ferrari produced 140 horsepower and the Lusso engine produced about 265 horsepower. The

The very attractive 1953 Farina bodied Nash Healy.

original 1953 version of the six-cylinder Nash Healy engine produced 140 horsepower, and this 1957 Nash Ambassador engine, with 327 cubic inch displacement, produced 255 horsepower and gobs of torque. This Nash Healy was *fast!* I also learned to appreciate Donald Healy's trailing link front suspension and the center point steering. Even driven very hard, the suspension and steering were outstanding for 1953. The weakest thing about the car now was the brakes. They were barely OK, certainly not up to the speed of which this car was now capable. The fourth gear overdrive was pretty tall, and while I never drove the car over 90, I imagine it would easily have done 135–140 and remained stable. I would like to have found a disc brake conversion kit for the car, to make the brakes safe, but I was never able to find one.

In 2000 I sold the Nash Healy to a collector in Salt Lake City for $45,000, a high price for that time, but a fair price for this one. They have since gone up in value and now bring that much or more for an unrestored car.

23

My Packard Education

Gene Rouse and I had become acquainted with Bill Parfet of Golden, Colorado, who had a small but very fine car collection, including a couple of contemporary Ferraris. Coors Ceramic Division in Golden made the space shuttle nose cone tiles using clay from Bill Parfet's mine. In about 1975 Gene bought a bastardized 1932 Packard from Bill, who was probably a good deal less than candid about it with Gene, who knew nothing about custom Packards. Originally it was a V-windshield Individual Custom Victoria, bodied by Ray Dietrich. Only a few custom-bodied Dietrich Packards had been sold during the Depression. Built on Packard's longest 144-inch wheelbase, they cost circa $6,000 at a time when a working man who was lucky enough to have a job earned an average of $750 a year! Moreover, many of these luxury cars were sold for scrap-metal during World War II. There was a saying among car dealers that "People who buy Packards don't buy used cars and people who buy used cars don't buy Packards." Even though ethyl gasoline was only twelve cents a gallon, big, thirsty cars were virtually worthless as used cars during the Depression. When this Packard was just a worthless used car, or perhaps in a junkyard, some unknown person had "customized" it by cutting it horizontally all the way through at the beltline from the radiator to the trunk, and sectioned it by about three inches. To lower it another two inches they also eliminated the big ash-wood sills on which the body bolted to the frame and welded in a flat sheet metal floor.

I was with Gene when he bought this car from Bill but paid little attention to it at the time because I wasn't interested in such cars. But in 1989–1990, when prices peaked, one or two of these rare Dietrich Packards had sold for over $600,000. Finding worthwhile cars to restore at a price that made economic sense had become very difficult. I was certain that Loran and I could restore the car and that if it cost no more than our other difficult restorations I might even make a good profit on it. I knew nothing about these custom Packards, but I knew the car was modified in other ways than just chopping the body to lower it. While owning my first Packard I saw photographs of the beautiful custom-bodied convertible Packards. I especially liked those built by Dietrich. Their length belied their size. The proportions were just plain elegant.

While we were visiting Gene, who had moved to Phoenix, he took the Packard out of storage so I could drive it, but it overheated and the steering was so crazy I just parked it. Gene didn't really know any more about the car than I did. I got the VIN, 904–95, and after going home I did more research about the Dietrich Packards. I bought it in May 1991 for $100,000 and had the car shipped to Fort Collins. Loran immediately began dismantling it.

Before starting work on the car I read the CCCA's rules regarding authenticity and their judging rules. They simply stated that any part of an original Classic car could be repaired or replaced as necessary to restore the car to its original condition so long as parts were from the same make, model and year. And if new parts were not available one could literally build a car from parts of other cars as long as one had at least part of the original car. To make matters worse, the CCCA regulations were unclear and in a state of flux at that time for the very reason that some members had been taking advantage of the lax rules. For example, the twelve-cylinder cars were worth much more than the eight-cylinder cars, and CCCA had allowed engine swapping as long as the chassis was the correct model and year. Then, the CCCA rules allowed swapping of a custom body to a different original chassis because a few original owners may have put their custom body on newer chassis.

After the car was apart we sent the frame, the body and most of the dismantled parts to Denver to have them sandblasted to the bare metal so we could see what had been done. The body had been cut about two inches below the beltline and the upper part dropped into the lower part, welded, ground smooth and filled with a huge amount of lead. Fortunately the metal was simply folded over, and was all there. Most of the body metal was in poor condition with a great deal of rust perforation, especially in the lower rear section of the body, called the "tub." The radiator had been ruined. The hood panels had also been shortened in height. I found that the instrument panel and steering wheel, the hydraulic brakes, wheels and both axles were also from a 1937 Packard and were unusable. All this was a major shock! I was not expecting that many modifications. But not to worry—they were worth so much when finished that I couldn't lose! Power steering had been added, which changed the steering linkage and geometry and was the reason it was so squirrelly. The engine was correct but carried a 1937 carburetor and manifold, plus the power steering pump modification. Externally, the taillights were from a later model and because the trunk had been cut through, the chrome trim was there but the locks were missing. The trunk rack was from a twelve-cylinder model and could not be used. The biggest shock of all was the convertible top bows. A later model padded power top had been converted to more or less fit the Packard, but it was completely wrong and could not be used. The whole car was an absolute mess. Naturally I was very concerned, but because these Dietrich Victorias were so valuable, I still felt sure I would come out OK financially.

Neither Loran nor I were ever secretive about what we were working on, but as it turned out, we should have been in this case. While the body was in Denver to be sandblasted, Zach Brinkerhoff saw it and found out what the car was. Zach called me and said he would like to buy the project from me. As things turned out I should have taken the money and run, but foolishly I told Zach I wanted to finish the car. This should have been a red flag, but I was too naïve to realize that some Classic Car (the capital C's are on purpose because it is a copyright name for the CCCA's approved classics) collectors are always hunting for an opportunity to find a "sleeper," and the cat was now out of the bag. I began to realize I might have stepped into an alien automobile world I knew nothing about. I needed some expert advice about how I should proceed with this tough project.

To determine what the original specifications were for these cars I turned to books and Packard experts for help. Perhaps the biggest help came from Richard Zerth, a CCCA member near Chicago who had a 1932 eight cylinder Dietrich Victoria that had just been judged 100 points at a National CCCA meeting. He was kind enough to allow me to come to his home and take about a hundred photographs of his car, in great detail, to guide us in our restoration. I also visited Fran Roxas, who had restored the Zerth car. His shop was in nearby Cicero. Fran had turned out a number of 100-point Classic Cars. Fran wasn't very hospitable, but while there I also met Chris Nerstheimer, who rented space from Fran and did the trim work on all of Fran's restorations. Chris is undoubtedly one of the best automotive upholsterers in the U.S. He did the interior and top on the Dietrich Victoria I had come to photograph. Chris said he would be glad to do my trim work when it was ready. The leather interior and convertible top on these custom cars were entirely different from the production cars, and Chris had the patterns. I was happy to know that a big part of my problem was solved. While there I also saw one of Fran's replica Le Baron Packard roadsters, and but for the firewall plate which clearly identified the car as a Fran Roxas Replica, even an expert could not tell it from an original. It was just stunning!

I then flew from Chicago to Oklahoma City to meet C.A. Leslie, who had written articles about the twelve-cylinder Packards. He said the CCCA rules would allow me to put my body on a twelve cylinder chassis, and that it would be worth 50 percent more if I did. He offered to sell me a twelve-cylinder parts car with all the accessory parts I would need to turn my original car into a twelve for $50,000. He agreed to give me $18,000 for my modified eight-cylinder engine and frame. Against my better judgment I let avarice take over and bought the stuff. Mr. Leslie had a large warehouse full of twelve-cylinder engines and parts. I inventoried the stuff and sent Loran back with my truck to Oklahoma City to pick it up. Soon after that, I read in the CCCA newsletter that the rules had changed and that my car must remain an eight-cylinder model as it was originally manufactured. I called Mr. Leslie about taking his stuff back and refunding my money, but he claimed he was unaware of the rules change and said that I should be able to sell the parts for at least as much as I paid for them.

I didn't believe Mr. Leslie misled me intentionally, but it turned into a disaster for me. I could only blame myself because I knew instinctively that a car should *always* remain what it was originally, and that based on all my previous experience the chassis frame number and the engine number were the essential proof of a car's originality. A CCCA board member who owned several Packards then advised that I could build as much of a new body as needed to properly restore my Dietrich Victoria.

In my search for information I learned of a very talented California man who was serving a prison term for stealing original parts from a car he was restoring for a customer. He kept the original parts and made replica parts for the customers' car. I never knew the details, but he had built a couple of replica Dietrich bodied Packard roadsters and apparently sold them as original cars. I was given the post office box number of the prisoner's wife. I wrote to her and she arranged for her husband to call me from prison. One of those replica cars was in the collection of a Las Vegas casino. Richie Clyne, the curator, allowed me to raise the hood to photograph certain details of the engine compartment. That was another car that was so well done it could easily have been sold as a genuine Dietrich Roadster. I could not call the man in prison but he could call me collect, which he did several times. He arranged for me to buy a set of replica bronze door hinges, a pair of door handle castings, the correct metal doorjamb plates and several big steel castings that bolted the wood doorjamb posts to the frame to support the big heavy doors. These parts were so critical I don't know how we could have done this job had I not found this source. There was nothing illegal about buying these reproduction parts. I would send the money to his wife's box number and she would ship the parts. I felt sorry for the man and his wife. I once asked him how long he had to serve, and he simply said "a long time." This illustrates what was beginning to happen as certain cars became so valuable that people were counterfeiting them and selling them as originals. This was the first and only time I ran into this situation. As I recall this man in prison, it reminds me how incredible some of these events were. All I was trying to do was restore a car!

I also called Robert Turnquist of Hibernia Restorations, who was a Packard authority and a prominent member of CCCA. He wrote the book *Packard* from which I had gotten a lot of information. He said it would be cheaper and faster to buy a spare parts car for all the parts I needed rather than trying to find the individual parts. The seven passenger formal sedans were also built on Packard's 144-inch chassis, and were among the least desirable, and therefore the least expensive at that time. From an ad in *Hemmings* I found a complete 1932 seven-passenger sedan and bought it for $35,000. We used only those parts that were missing from the Dietrich, intending to sell off the rest, but since we now had the wood patterns and doorjambs and hinges, and the original windshield castings, Loran suggested building a replica Dietrich Victoria at the same time we were restoring the original car. This made some sense at the time. There is nothing immoral or illegal about building good replica cars so long as they are clearly identified as such. Fran Roxas' Packard Le Baron replica roadsters sold for $400,000. Based on the prevailing prices for perfect replicas, I agreed to build a replica because doing two at once would lower the unit cost for a lot of things we had to make. And all this happened before we actually got far into working on my car!

Loran hammered the body metal back to its original height and tack-welded it enough to rebuild the wood frame, which was almost entirely missing. I called around until I found Gene Irvine, who made new wood for old cars. Unbelievably, he had once made new wood for a Dietrich Victoria and had kept the old wood for patterns in case they were ever needed again! He *rented* the patterns to me with a cash deposit to ensure their return. These bodies depend on the shape of the wood framing to define the shape of the body. After Loran finished the wood for both bodies I hauled the chassis frame and the original body to Corona, California, for Marcel DeLey and his two sons to finish the metal work on the original car, and to build a second identical replica body. Meanwhile, we rebuilt the engines and running gear of the two cars. I had met Marcel years before

The original wood and metal in the cowl. Jackie talks to one of Marcel's sons. The left photograph shows where the body metal was cut below the beltline.

The new metal side panels of the cowl and the whole new rear "tub" of the body.

when he was in Orange County. He had immigrated to the U.S. from Belgium when the custom body business all but ceased in Europe after the war. His two sons were now grown and trained in the highly skilled craft. These fine craftsmen refused to repair bad panels, and made a whole new tub and side cowl panels. I insisted they retain the top of the cowl metal because the only original wood was attached underneath it and the bronze windshield posts were hand-fitted to the cowl, and we had to have some of the original metal to meet the CCCA rules.

Loran built an angle iron jig to hold the body to its proper shape while

Every detail of the engine is perfect. We machined the rods for insert bearing shells.

the wood and metal work was finished. Rust had perforated the metal around the vent door opening on the underside of the cowl. According to the CCCA rules there was no reason why new metal panels should not be made to replace the rusted out tub. The original fenders were still good, needing no significant repairs.

Whoever modified this car changed the doors to hinge from the front instead of from the rear. This changed the doorjambs, which proved to be difficult to correct, requiring the new bronze hinges and jambs I bought from the convict. The body was mounted to heavy ash-wood sills. It was exciting for me to see all our research and eighteen months of hard work coming together into something tangible! I had ordered six new chrome wheels to be built by Don Sommer in Michigan, at a cost of $1,200 each. We used the wheels from the parts car while we were working on the bodies, then had those wheels rebuilt and chrome plated for the second car.

When the bodies came back to our shop, Loran painted the chassis frame and began assembling the engine, transmission and all the components he had rebuilt while waiting for the body to be finished. I met Don Sears of Omaha. He owned an original Dietrich Convertible Sedan and

Details like these make the difference in a 100-point car.

was helpful by making small parts duplicated from his car. I wish I had met Don before I ever started this project.

I had the rods machined for insert bearings. An aircraft shop balanced the engine. I chose the paint and trim colors very carefully. The car I had photographed was all dark blue with a white top. I knew these Dietrich-built cars were not quite as formal as the production cars, so I chose a medium dark gray-green for the chassis frame and fenders with a light gray body. The top material was selected to match the fender color as closely as possible. The interior leather was ivory. I was shooting for a 100-point car. The difference between, say, a 98 point car and a 100-point car is in a myriad of fine details, like correct engraving on the headlights, the interior ashtrays, the correct instrument panel finish and a highly finished undercarriage. I spent a great deal of time and money sending many things out to have these details done by specialists.

All the trim and small hardware items on the custom built Dietrich cars were different from those used on the production cars, so every item that was missing on the original car became a challenge. Just finding two of the smoking vanities, in poor condition, for $300 was reason to celebrate!

The rear seats and convertible top show Chris Nerstheimer's fine workmanship.

Having water-jet cut stainless steel door-lock assemblies made for $500 was reason to sleep well that night! And we gave thanks for the specialist that does nothing but the proper pattern of wood graining for instrument panels. The headlight rims had to be re-engraved before being chrome-plated. This type of detail is lost in the metal polishing process before the plating is done. The engraving is but one tiny detail of the sort that judges look for in a 100-point car, because that's the way the car came from the factory. The instruments were all rebuilt with new faces and chrome plated bezels. And the undercarriage of the car is almost as highly finished as the body. Every nut and bolt must be the proper type and size to ensure the car passes the most discriminating judge's scrutiny. And of course the engine had better start instantly and settle into a quiet purr.

The top bows were still a major problem. I believe the restoration gods meant for me to finish this Dietrich Victoria, for I learned that another

The finished Individual Dietrich Victoria Packard, No. 904–95.

shop in California was restoring a Dietrich Victoria. That was amazing, considering that there were only four 1932 eight cylinder models known, and less than a dozen of all models. I called to get permission to fly out to photograph and measure the top bows. The shop owner was very reluctant to allow me to do this until he was convinced I was not trying to build a counterfeit. I also had to pay him $50 an hour to come in over a weekend but I got what I needed to have the wood bows made and for Loran to machine all the metal parts. When these parts were finished the car could then to go to Chris Nerstheimer for the interior and cloth top. Chris had moved his shop to Scottsdale, Arizona. I personally delivered the car to Chris in my own truck. His work cost about $16,000 but the results speak for themselves.

It was important to show the Packard and have it judged in a Concour d'Élégance in order to maximize its value. I was invited to bring the car to Pebble Beach. We had to rush to complete it by the end of August 1994. I drove the car enough to tune it as best as I could in the short time we had. The engine and drivetrain was excellent, but there was a problem with the brakes, and even though he spent a week, and dismantled the

Crossing the ramp and accepting the prize at Pebble Beach.

mechanical brakes several times, Loran could not find the problem. When the brakes were applied, they would not stop the car as they should, and would suddenly grab, locking up the rear wheels. I found that I could usually unlock the back wheels by reversing the car. We were out of time so I had Loran deliver it to Pebble Beach and hope for the best. Other than the brakes, it was absolutely elegant!

The car took second place at Pebble Beach in the Convertible Packard class. It was beat out for first place because of some slight blemishes in the paint on the hood, which we did not have time for Loran to correct before leaving for California. First place was won by Zach Brinkerhoff's Model 902 standard convertible Phaeton, restored by Mark Clayton, of Castle Rock, Colorado. It was absolutely perfect!

I was disappointed that our car had not taken first place, but I had to admit that the paint-work on Zach's car was better. While Zach's car was an ordinary production model Phaeton, that made no difference in the class in which both cars were entered. I was pleased when Strother MacMinn, the long-time instructor of automotive styling at Art Center in Los Angeles, brought a couple of students by to see what he called a "truly elegant car." Several professional stylists from Chrysler also admired the car.

It had been a long, stressful and tiring day for me, getting the car on the field very early in the morning. When I was called to take the car over the winner's award ramp, I started the drive to the ramp when the damned brakes locked up again! Jackie and our daughters, Robin and Jennifer, who had flown to California just for Pebble Beach, were with me in the car. I tried backing up but they did not unlock. I had to put the car in low and move the car with the brakes locked. I could smell the clutch getting hot, and I was furious at Loran for not finding the trouble and fixing the brakes the week before we left! I got the car onto the ramp and Jackie received the trophy. I took the car from the field even though we were not supposed to leave that soon.

Loran had brought the car to California in my covered trailer. He loaded the car and left immediately. He knew that I was very upset about the brakes, but I didn't say anything at the time. We were staying in the beautiful Lodge at Pebble Beach for the first time and I did not want to spoil our vacation. Our daughters were in a nearby motor lodge and we had a wonderful few days in the area visiting the Aquarium at Fisherman's Wharf, sampling the fine seafood restaurants and driving down the Big Sur.

When we returned home, Loran and I had a long, serious talk about his work. He admitted that he was getting tired of restoring cars and that the Packard had been especially hard for him because the rules regarding authenticity and judging regulations for Classic Cars were things he knew nothing about. Too much of the research and finding solutions to problems had fallen on me. He had been working for me, or my company, for almost twenty years. Loran was a gifted craftsman, justifiably proud of his work, but he was not capable of doing that part of the restoration work that I had contributed. We had worked as a team, but I was getting old and tired too. It was a sad parting, but when I told Loran I would at least like to part as friends, he said he wouldn't have it any other way.

Jackie's brother, Jerry Munson, had retired from a career as a professional trumpet player in Las Vegas. When his wife died Jerry came to live near us in Fort Collins. Jerry had always been interested in my cars and before he retired had made a part-time business of rebuilding and repairing the engines of modern Alfa Romeos. I had the Dietrich Packard at home, and on a weekend, we decided to put it up on floor stands and see if we could fix the brakes. Reading the manual carefully we soon discovered the problem. When the brake pedal was pressed, a pivot on a cross-shaft operated rods that went forward to the front brakes, and rods that went backward to the rear brakes. The rods operated small levers on the brake backer plates and they had simply been hooked up wrong. It took about thirty minutes to sort it out and fix it. The brakes were then very good and powerful. The Packard was finally finished. I drove it for pleasure for almost two years before I sold it. The engine was especially smooth and powerful, and the car was a delight to drive. The steering was surprisingly light. After the engine was broken in I was pleasantly surprised at how fast the car was. It had an optional high-speed rear axle ratio that made a great difference in the overall character of the car. Usually, low gear in these cars were only good for pulling tree stumps, but with this axle ratio, low was a practical first gear and third was an excellent ratio for modern driving. I can highly recommend a high-speed ring and pinion for anyone considering changing the axle ratio on a Classis Packard or other similar car.

Rebuilding the second Packard that we intended to be a replica of the first car turned into a nightmare. In March of 1993, when we brought the rebuilt cowl and the new tub of the original body plus the second replica body back from Macel DeLey, they also sent the old rusty sheet metal from the tub. Loran crushed it flat and put it outside to be thrown away.

Several months later a man, who shall remain nameless, came to see our almost completed Dietrich Victoria. He asked if I would sell the replica body, the parts we had made and acquired for the replica car and all the twelve-cylinder parts. He said he wanted to build a twelve-cylinder replica. I decided to sell the replica project because the first one had taken so long and had been so difficult. They comprised about half of a complete car. I sold him everything for my cost to date of $112,000 plus our costs to deliver them to Michigan so he didn't have to crate and ship them. Before he left, he asked if he could have the old sheet metal tub we were going to throw away. He said he might be able to use it for patterns. It being worthless to us, we gave it to him.

We heard nothing from him for a year or more, then, shortly after I returned with my restored car from Pebble Beach, I received a letter from the Chairman of the CCCA committee stating that the man had applied to the committee for approval of a Dietrich Victoria, Number 904–95! *My car!* I was asked to defend my claim of ownership of the *same car!* I immediately consulted my attorney. This, to me, was a clear case of attempted fraud. The only thing the man had from the original car was the old sheet metal tub—which we had given to him—and the replica parts we had made. Even after fifty years of all the vagaries in business I have never been so totally blind-sided. After all our efforts to restore this car as best we possibly could, and seeking the advice of a number of so-called experts,

Jerry Munson in the convertible Packard. The big car makes him look small.

I could not believe a CCCA member was trying to steal my car using cronyism and the ill-defined and constantly changing rules of the CCCA to do so!

My attorney and I wrote a detailed reply in which we outlined the entire history of the car, from the time Gene Rouse bought it from Bill Parfet, to the completion of the car. We stated that we had the original transmission, the cowl, the only original sheet metal that was deemed usable, including the fenders, headlights, bumpers, the hood, the trunk, the doors and the top of the cowl, with the only usable pieces of original wood. Everything we had done was sanctioned by the CCCA rules. We also had the original bronze windshield castings, stamped with the number 904–95, and most important, we had the original firewall-plate from the factory, with the car's VIN number, 904–95, with the date of delivery and the Packard dealer who sold the car originally.

The CCCA president intervened to present our letter to the full Board of Directors when they next met, after which they would give their decision. This matter was very important because the CCCA was the ultimate authority on Packards, and if they should not rule in my favor, my car would go from a $600,000 car to a replica worth about $150,000! I did not ask to attend because my attorney felt certain they could not possibly rule against me. *But they did!* The other man was well known to all the Board members and he appeared in person, while I relied on my attorney's letter and the common sense of the Board members for a ruling in my favor.

I immediately filed suit for fraud in the Federal Court in Colorado. The man worked for a big corporation in a middle management position.

Our investigation showed him living in an up-scale neighborhood, with an affluent lifestyle. He tried unsuccessfully to have the venue changed. He had to hire a Denver attorney from a prestigious law firm, and my attorney advised me to retain an equally prestigious law firm in Fort Collins. Not just any attorney practices before the federal courts. We went through two years of discoveries and depositions, for which he had to fly to Denver each time these were taken.

Here I must say that the CCCA is one of the oldest and most highly respected car clubs in America. There have been, and still are, countless unselfish people that have made it so. Quite a number of these members helped me a great deal. But, like any large organization, there were a few self-serving men in high positions, and probably some cronyism that made this unfortunate situation possible. C.A. Leslie's bad advice got me off on the wrong foot. The frequent changes in the club's rules during that time period were confusing and unclear. What happened was due to the incredible increase in value of some Classic Cars. Similar things have happened with other makes, particularly some Ferraris. Next to Duesenbergs these Dietrich Packards were among the most desirable and valuable American Classics. I also have to take responsibility for my naïveté and ignorance about Classic Cars. The value of a Packard depends largely on winning a CCCA National First Senior badge, and to compete the car must be accepted as an authentic Classic, according to CCCA rules. It was a catch–22 situation because CCCA is the only game in town for a Packard.

The discoveries and depositions taken under oath proved that, even before coming to Colorado on the pretense of buying my replica project, this man had written to the CCCA committee chairman for an opinion. In that letter he said he knew of part of a Dietrich Victoria, consisting of the sheet metal tub, some of the wood and a twelve-cylinder chassis. He asked if he bought it, and built a car around those parts, if it would be sanctioned as an authentic car. He was told that it would, but not as a Twelve under the new CCCA rules. At an exorbitant price he then quietly bought the frame and the original modified eight-cylinder engine I had traded to C.A. Leslie on the twelve-cylinder parts car. (Even though I spoke to Mr. Leslie frequently he never said anything to me about it.) Only then did the man buy our parts, and with intent to defraud, had us give him the old sheet metal tub. I had some previous experience in the federal courts when we had to sue a Canadian company for patent infringement, so I was not naïve about that! The federal courts move exceedingly slowly, and a suit is exceedingly expensive. After two years of depositions and discoveries, and pressure from the overloaded judge, we agreed to arbitrate. I refunded his money, got all my parts back, including the sheet metal tub, and we each paid our own attorney fees. Mine were about $75,000 but I'm sure his were much more.

As usual in litigation, no one won, but I simply could not let him get away with defrauding me. This episode led to a complete revision and clarification of the CCCA rules, but my advice to anyone working on anything less than a complete, unmodified, unquestionable car is to submit it to the committee before the restoration even begins. This experience soured me regarding the CCCA. I dropped my membership and will always remember this as the one and only really bad experience I ever had buying, restoring or selling a collectible car.

When we got it back I turned over the second Packard that Loran had started to Mark Clayton to finish. His fine work had beaten my car at Pebble Beach. Since the CCCA had ruled the second car was the authentic Dietrich Victoria, Mark had to weld the old tub into the new body built by Marcel DeLey. This meant relegating my first Packard to the status of a replica, so I let the CCCA ruling stand. Mark Clayton was a pleasure to work with. He is diligent, honest, does excellent work and his prices are fair. He is also an expert on Packards and other Classics, having restored a number of 100-point cars. He is active in the various car clubs and attends

The second Packard chassis in Mark Clayton's shop.

The CCCA 100 point Dietrich Victoria, now designated 904–95.

the regional and national CCCA meetings. If I had hired him to restore the car to begin with none of this would have happened.

I turned over the original VIN plate, 904–95, for Mark to attach to this firewall. I was so disgusted with this Packard experience that I lost all interest in the cars and only kept the first Packard long enough for Mark to complete this car and to have him show it to prove the quality of the car. I had Mark take it to a national CCCA meet in Dallas where it scored 100 points and won its First Junior badge. I went with him to the next CCCA national meeting in Albuquerque, where it again scored 100 points and received its First Senior body badge. At least, I had achieved the goal of making it a 100-point car.

I showed the gray car at a national Antique Automobile Club of America show in Cheyenne, where it was judged first in class. I sold it in 1996, designated as a replica with 904–00 on its VIN plate, for only $125,000, a net loss of $140,000. And because of all the bad publicity about the cars the second car was tainted in the eyes of some. I never even drove that car on the road and sold it in 1997 for only $350,000 for another loss of $42,000. While the market for such cars went down after 1990, if the man had not tried to steal the rights to my car these two cars would have been worth at least $750,000 and I would have made a small profit of at least $90,000 for the incredible amount of effort, time and money I invested.

The Dietrich bodied cars are now even more valuable than they were in 1989–1990. Now, fifteen years after the lawsuit and with the bad publicity forgotten, whoever owns each of these Packards has a very fine car that was honestly restored to the very highest standards. But if I made a choice for a car to drive, I'd take the gray car.

Today, judged objectively on their own merits, this pair of cars would easily bring $900,000 or more.

24

The Austin
Mini Cooper S

With nothing to keep him occupied Jackie's brother Jerry soon became bored. He also needed some extra income to augment his Social Security. After I recovered from the initial trauma of the Packard episode Jerry and I thought it would be fun to work together restoring another car. Jerry was very good with engines but had never restored a car before, and was reluctant to work on anything like my former projects he had been familiar with. In our business travels, Jackie and I had always visited Jerry and his wife Ginger whenever we were in Las Vegas. The electric sign industry naturally held many national association trade shows in Las Vegas. Ginger was a professional dancer when they met, and Jerry worked in the relief band. Jerry and Ginger had worked all the big show rooms. The regular hotel bands only get one night off a week, and the relief bands played on their night off, so the relief band worked a different show every night. This required musicians that could sight-read any music set before them, and they usually got only one rehearsal before they played for some of the biggest names in show business in those days. Musicians in the relief band were paid a lot more than scale.

Jackie and I have many fond memories of taking in a show where Jerry was playing, then meeting him between shows or after the late show at 1:00 AM. Jerry knew the town intimately, and where the best food was almost free! We would hit some of the lounge shows, where in the old days big name bands and musicians played. Just imagine listening to Harry James or Stan Kenton in a *lounge show!* Jerry had a wonderful career like very few musicians have. He lived in one place, and even though the hours were topsy-turvy, they were regular, steady hours. Ginger retired from show business when she had her first child. They raised two kids in Las Vegas. I always took Jerry some photos of what I was restoring, so he was very familiar with the work we had done. A lot of musicians are "car guys" so some of the other men in the band were glad to see the latest pictures of my current projects.

I thought it would be good for Jerry to have the experience, but I also thought it would be best to begin with a simple project. I used to say that I could enjoy restoring a Model A Ford just as much as restoring an expensive car because I derived my satisfaction by meeting the challenges and in seeing the project coming together, then testing the finished car. That was an exaggeration, however, and because I was hooked on foreign cars, I never gave serious consideration to restoring a Model A Ford. I didn't have to think long to decide what it should be: a Mini Cooper S was just the thing. It was simple, but also a worthwhile car to restore, meaning that I should be able to break even on it when it was finished and when I might want to sell it.

I also had fond memories of the Mini Cooper S as one of the most fun cars I ever owned. It was a 1967 model that I bought in about 1978. I would load Arlen Goodwine, two other six-foot-plus employees and myself and go to lunch. We would pick somewhere we could park by the restaurant and be seen getting out of the car. It was a little like watching the clown act in the circus where a never ending stream of clowns seem to emerge from one side of their trick car while others are going around to the other side and getting in again. People would see my front seat passenger and me emerge; when we stood up, the top of the car would be about waist high. The two rear seat passengers would then come out and we would all stand beside the car. People who knew nothing about Minis found it hard to believe that four big men could get into such a tiny car. That always set the mood for a fun lunch break. If the people in the restaurant saw our comedic act someone would invariably make a comment or ask a question about the Mini, and if Arlen Goodwine was there he immediately went into his Terry Thomas exaggerated British accent. Having spent most of his youth in England, he could do it perfectly. He even had a minor version of Terry Thomas' gap in his front teeth as well as a knife-sharp wit. He would give an impromptu spiel about the British Mini Cooper.

The fact was that once we were in the car we all had plenty of room. The Minis were almost all passenger space. The front doors were big and the seats were low. The roof height and legroom were adequate for very tall people. The little four-cylinder Austin engine sits smack over the front wheels. It is mounted transversely with the transmission integrated into the crankcase. This leaves the floor perfectly flat and close to the ground because there is no drive shaft or differential.

As a designer I used to think about originality, or thinking "outside the box." We are preconditioned by what already is and find it difficult to think of something in a totally different way. Alexander (Alex) Issigonis had the unique gift of thinking outside the box and therefore was able to design a truly new concept of an automobile. Born in Smyrna, now a part of Turkey, he never saw a car until he was ten years old. His family owned a boiler factory. His mother took him to London to study engineering when he was sixteen, and upon graduation he went to work for the British auto industry.

As project manager for Morris Motors he designed a small, front-wheel drive car that developed into the Morris Minor that was in production from 1948 through 1971. Morris merged with Austin in 1952. During the Suez crisis and gas rationing Issigonis was given the task of designing a new small car capable of carrying four full size people, using an existing four-cylinder Austin engine. It was revolutionary in that he placed the engine transversely and integrated the transmission in the bottom of the engine. With wheels of only ten-inch diameter, placed out on each corner, with a very wide stance for the size of the car, it was extremely stable. The suspension system was by rubber cones for each wheel. It was launched in 1959 with an Austin engine of only 850cc developing 34 horsepower. The engine displacement grew from that to 997cc and 55 horsepower and finally to 1275cc and 76 horsepower.

John Cooper was a two-time Formula I World Champion Constructor who became the "Cooper" in the Mini Cooper name. He breathed life into the little car, and his Works team cars produced 91 bhp. In that guise they won the Monte Carlo Rally four years straight, 1964–1967. They became a "must have" status symbol among such people as The Beatles, Peter Sellers, Graham Hill and even Enzo Ferrari, who drove one for his everyday car! In its various iterations it remained in production through 2000. The significance of the Mini was such that Alex Issigonis was knighted by the Queen, just as was Sir William Lyons of Jaguar for his contribution to the British economy. But knighthood never changed Issigonis' mind about what a small car should be. He believed an economy car should be very spartan, having no radio, fancy seats or much concern for creature comfort. And that certainly describes the Austin Mini Cooper S. They just ran like hell! I don't believe you could turn one over if you tried.

Jerry Munson did the dismantling and all the mechanical restoration

The small but mighty 1275cc engine of the 1967 Austin Mini Cooper S.

of my last Mini. We stripped it down to the bare metal body. I painted it inside and out and Jerry began putting it back together as he finished each component. Parts are no problem; Moss Motors can provide any part needed for most British sports cars.

We even ordered the correct engine enamel colors from Moss, and with all new parts it made as cute an engine compartment as anyone could want. The water radiator was located on the left side of the engine compartment. As part of the Cooper additions, it also had an oil cooler in front of the engine, behind a removable grill. The transmission was integrated into the engine sump and was lubricated from a common oil supply. These cars had an almighty torque-steer that would tend to turn the car to the right when you accelerated hard. Later front-wheel drive automobiles corrected this somewhat via unequal length half-shafts.

I couldn't resist upgrading the interior a bit compared to my first '67 Mini Cooper, which had such a poor grade of vinyl upholstering that every time I left the car outdoors with the windows up, the plasticizer in the vinyl out-gassed so much it left a film on the windshield. This time I used a top grade Naugahyde, pleated the seats and enhanced the side door trim. We also had better grade carpets made. We replaced all the rubber trim

The oil cooler fitted behind the removable grill.

The new and improved interior trim was nothing fancy but more so than the original.

on the car as well. I had no intention of keeping this car very long, but drove it enough to seat the rings and be sure everything was perfect. Once again, I was impressed with what wonderful little cars they were. As can be seen by the steering wheel position, the column was much more verti-

The finished Mini Cooper S, a world-famous favorite of the cognoscenti.

cal than in most cars, somewhat like that of a bus. One is inclined to lean over the steering wheel a bit. There isn't a lot of chrome plating on a Mini but we replaced or replated what there was. The car had the custom wheels shown when I bought it from a fellow in Phoenix that built Cobra replica kits. He had intended to restore the car but never found the time.

With the Mini Cooper Jerry had shown that he was meticulous and careful as he went. He didn't have to do things over because he would read the manuals until he understood his task before he began. He also was more confident after seeing that restoration work was not much different from engine work. Essentially it is a matter of totally dismantling a car, sorting and storing things in some sort of order, and where uncertainty is possible, taking photographs as things are dismantled. All restorers have their own methods, but once the car is dismantled, it becomes a sequence of cleaning, inspecting, crack testing if deemed important, rebuilding, refinishing, plating and re-assembling the whole car progressively until it is finished.

When I was ready to sell the Mini Cooper I ran an ad in the *Denver Post* and sold the car to a man and his college student son from an upscale neighborhood in Denver. The man had once owned a Mini Cooper and wanted his son to appreciate what they were all about. Obviously, he was really a good dad.

25

The Twelve-Cylinder Pierce Arrow Club Brougham

The twelve-cylinder Pierce Arrow as I bought it in Connecticut.

When I was ready to put Jerry to work on a serious restoration I remembered what a nice car my eight-cylinder Pierce Arrow had been and began looking for a twelve-cylinder Club Brougham, a very pretty body style. They were very hard to find, but I finally bought one for $17,500, a car with the wrong twelve-cylinder engine that had been stored outdoors in Connecticut for years, with a badly leaking top.

One might ask why we began with such a rough car that needed virtually everything, and was also incomplete. The answer is the rarity of the body style. But it was also another work of love. Passport hauled the car to Fort Collins and we began the usual appraisal of everything it needed as we dismantled it. Barely enough of the interior was intact to use for patterns. It would be a major project. I was seventy-two years old and Jerry was sixty-seven, so we only worked about four or five hours a day. I paid Jerry his hourly rate that he had charged for working on modern Alfas in Las Vegas.

Wire wheels were an option when the car was new, and because the original wheels were badly rusted I found six wire wheels and a proper 1933 engine for $7,500, all needing rebuilding. New reproduction hubcaps came from Bill Hirsch. The chrome plating for this car would be a major cost. Even though there was not a lot of chrome on the car, other than the big radiator shell and louvers that were so prominent on the Pierce Arrows, those were in bad shape. Regardless of the amount of polishing and copper plating to build up the shell and louvers, they would never be of top show quality. The total chrome-plating work cost almost $6,000.

Jerry concentrated on the mechanical work while I farmed out everything we could not do. We hauled the body to Mark Gillespie in the little village of Howard, Colorado, almost 200 miles from our shop. Mark would do the bodywork, and his friend Stan Willoughby would do the paintwork. There were several very well qualified people in Howard as a result of a prominent car restoration shop there. The body and paint work cost $8,300.

We shipped the engine to Harkins Machine shop in Watertown, South Dakota. Mr. Harkins had done the engine machine work for a number of my cars because he had all the old machines and equipment to cast his own babbitt bearings and for align-boring the old engines. Pierce Arrows were one of the first to use hydraulic valve lifters. These parts were not available but fortunately we found that Cadillac lifters could be used. The car weighed almost 6,000 pounds, and to ensure adequate braking, Pierce Arrow had developed a mechanical power brake system, driven off the transmission. We lucked out in this regard because the transmission was still in good condition.

Jerry rebuilt the brakes and began assembling the engine when it was returned from Harkins. I was kept busy using all the sources and contacts I knew for rebuilding the accessories and obtaining new pistons, valves and guides as well as a myriad of small services such as instrument work; rebuilding the generator, starter, distributor, and carburetor; having the porcelain exhaust manifold redone; finding the proper gaskets; and having a new exhaust system and a new wiring harness made. I also painted all the small components such as the wheels and engine parts. We painted the chassis black, its original color. I chose the body colors from a Mercedes paint book because they had such nice, conservative metallic colors.

We had a problem when we first ran the engine. It started easily but took quite a while to build up oil pressure in the hydraulic lifters. We let the engine run at about 1800 rpm for about thirty minutes with a large floor fan in front of the radiator. The engine slowed and stopped. When we tried to restart it, it was too tight to crank. We discovered that the line we had drilled and tapped for a Fram oil filer had partially blocked the oil flow. Fearing we had damaged the engine, we pulled it and shipped it back to Harkins in South Dakota to rebuild again as necessary. Jerry was having some health problems so I had Harkins do the engine reassembly this

The power brake system was driven off the transmission.

time. This was a costly error we made, in both time and money. Because Jerry was unable to work, I sent the car to Mark Clayton to remove the engine. He had to dismantle the radiator and most of the front end of the body to pull the engine. He also reinstalled the engine when it was returned from Harkins.

When the car was finished except for the interior upholstering, we took it to Auto Weave in Denver to match the original patterns and style. I chose the best quality fabrics that closely matched the original. The interior trim work cost $6,100. All the door and windshield moldings were sent to a specialist for wood graining. New safety glass was installed in the windows and windshield. Auto Weave did a fine job and the interior was beautiful!

Boiling out and sealing the gas tank is standard practice when restoring an old car that has been out of service for some time. They are always rusty and will clog up the gas lines and carburetor. We did this with the Pierce Arrow, but we had to do it a second time because some debris

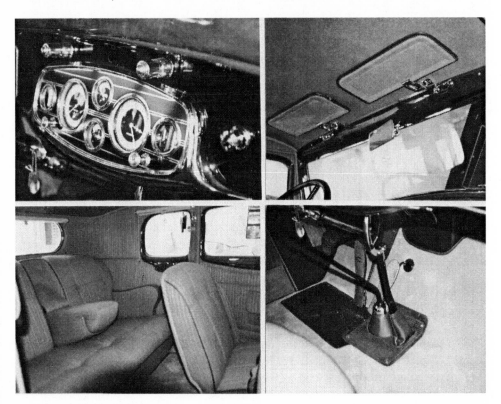

Refinished instrument panel, wood trim and complete new interior upholstery.

The restored 1933 Pierce Arrow Club Brougham.

escaped the rubber-like sealant that is poured into the tank, which is turned and rolled until all the surfaces have been coated. It is then allowed to cure, which permanently seals the inside of the gas tank. The problem this time was that the sealant was not suitable for gasoline that had ethanol content, even though the manufacturer advertised it to be so.

Another correction I chose to make was to have new ring and pinion gears made for the rear axle. The 1933 Pierce Twelve has a worm drive, with a very low gear ratio, which makes modern highway speeds unpleasant because the engine is turning at almost its maximum rpm range. This is a major undertaking, requiring swapping a rear axle from the eight-cylinder Pierce, to make a higher ratio ring and pinion possible. I purchased a used rear axle and shipped it to Eric Rosenau in California. I paid for the tooling for a high-speed ring and pinion gear set made by B & R Machine & Gear in one of the southern states. The cost for the eight-cylinder axle, the tooling and making the gear-set, the freight and the labor for all this was about $8,500. But it made a totally different driving car. I was concerned that the gear ratio might be too high for the Pierce engine to pull the heavy car up a mountain grade in high gear, but I tested it by pulling a very long, steep grade in high gear, and while the engine was working hard, I never had to down-shift.

The completion of the Pierce Arrow coincided with Mark Clayton finishing and showing the Packard. He hauled the Packard and Pierce

Arrow to Albuquerque for the regional National CCCA judging. I had no intention of having the Pierce judged, but it attracted so much attention, the chief judge asked me to have it judged. I relented. It placed second, to my Packard's First Place.

In 1997 I placed an illustrated, full-page ad in *Hemmings* and sold the Pierce Arrow to Richard and Patricia Donahey of Bellville, Michigan, for less than my cost. He had Mark deliver it directly to Michigan in time for a 200 mile CCCA Tour. It had cost $18,000 more than I sold it for, not counting the many hours of my time. But I had restored it to my own satisfaction and I enjoyed working on the car with Jerry Munson, who never recovered from his illness.

I was pleased when Phil Hill called me to ask permission to have a high-speed ring and pinion gear set made for his own Pierce Arrow. The gear company would not make those gears for anyone else without my permission because I had paid for the initial tooling. I gladly gave the gear company written permission to make the high-speed ring and pinion, not only for Phil but also for any owner of a Pierce Arrow that wanted one. This was a small favor in return for his driving my 6C-1750 Alfa Romeo at Laguna Seca in 1985.

When Jerry died I was seventy-four years old. I had no reason or ambition to restore another car. I had other interests to keep me occupied. Although I was completely retired from our company I still did the design work and wrote technical and advertising copy and did the layout for our considerable volume of literature. I designed the homes we lived in. I still read a lot. There was always something I could do, but in spite of all this, I was easily bored. From time to time I thought about buying a restored car to drive on one of the Classic Car tours. Those tours are one of the best things the CCCA does for its members who want to drive their cars. Once or twice a year there are short tours in one's own region, usually over three days. Then there are the national tours of about ten days' duration. They really go first class, through scenic and historical parts of the country, staying in some of the most beautiful and historical hotels and lodges. More important than just driving one's car is the social interaction with the other people on these tours. These tours are so attractive and popular that one has to sign up quickly when the next tour is announced by the tour committee chairman. Many CCCA members have become regulars on these national tours and the number of cars is limited so it is not always easy to "make the cut." My unhappy experience with one of the CCCA members spoiled the national tour idea because he always made those trips, and I knew Jackie and I would not enjoy being around him.

I waxed hot and cold about buying restored cars. I knew I was getting to an age where there would always be the uncertainty of my ability to care for them and in case I was disabled or should die, I didn't want to leave the matter of liquidating valuable cars up to my family. Boredom won out. I decided to buy a small group of interesting cars that were not too valuable, that should be easy to sell when the time came, and that should always bring as much or more than they cost. I built a new metal building on our commercial property, large enough for six cars and a workspace.

I wanted to have the same models of cars that I had owned before and would enjoy having again, or possibly cars that best represented their country of origin. I knew myself well enough to know that I would probably never be satisfied with any car I bought and would always find something that needed fixing. But that was OK. I wanted something I could tend to even if I could no longer work on them myself. I had come to respect Mark Clayton, and we had become friends, although Mark was the same age as my oldest grandson. Mark assured me he would do any work I needed on my cars. Eventually I acquired a supercharged Cord, a British Alvis Speed 25, another French Citroën SM, the black XKE Jaguar roadster, a German Mercedes 280 SL roadster, a Nash Healy roadster made in the U.S., the U.K. and Italy, and a Ferrari 400i. First came the Cord.

26

The 1937 Supercharged Cord Phaeton

I don't know which is more interesting, Cord the man or Cord the automobile. I'll start with the man. He was different to say the least. He made a huge fortune, the foundation of which was made building automobiles that were different, deliberately aimed at a niche market share. While still in high school he bought used Model T Fords, which were almost always black, for about ten dollars, painted them different colors and sold them for a good profit. He parlayed that into a string of garages and that into a bus line that went broke. He arrived in Chicago in 1919 at the age of 24 with $50 to his name and went to work selling Moon automobiles. In five years he had saved $100,000 and was so successful selling Moons that he was made a partner in the dealership. His marketing genius attracted some Chicago bankers who wanted him to take over the floundering Auburn Automobile Company in Auburn, Indiana, with stock options. There were hundreds of unattractive, unsold cars at the factory and in dealers' inventories. Remembering his Model T's, he repainted them in snappy two-color combinations and sold every one, creating much needed cash. He introduced styling at a time when most American cars were not much more than boxes on wheels, and Auburns became good sellers. Wanting his cars to be exciting, he bought the Lycoming engine works, produced an eight-cylinder engine that made the cars fast as well as good looking, and priced them well below what the public expected to pay for such automobiles. He soon owned the company. He bought the Duesenberg brothers' company, thereby acquiring their name, reputation and racing engine expertise. In 1929 he introduced the new Duesenberg, America's most expensive automobile. He also bought the rights from Miller for the design of his front-wheel-drive racecars. He then introduced the low-slung front-wheel-drive Cord L-29 that had some of the best-looking bodies ever put on an American car. Excepting its styling, it was not a very good car because of unresolved technical problems for passenger cars with front-wheel drive. The L-29 was the first car to carry the Cord name, but it ceased production after three years.

E. L. Cord put all his eggs into his holding company that also owned an airline, a steamship company and much, much more. The depression and the S.E.C. temporarily clipped his wings. But E.L. Cord wasn't hurt much. His buying and selling of stock in his own companies would be highly illegal today. He went back to California, made another fortune in real estate then another in uranium in the fifties. He went into politics in Nevada where he became a state senator. Without question he was a mover and shaker!

Now, regarding Cord the automobile. The introduction of the 810 Cord in 1936 caused a sensation at the New York Automobile Show. It was miraculous that it even made the show, as it was not completely finished. Needing to conduct further development, the company could not fill all the orders they took at the show, and matters were made worse by the competition's campaign of rumors, some true, most not true. The company was literally going into receivership when the supercharged 812 Cords were built in 1937. Only 196 were built before the doors were closed in August 1937, so their rarity was guaranteed. Some have said the car was just too advanced for its time, and without question it pushed the envelope of automotive technology, but there was nothing wrong with the car that would not have been corrected and improved with a little more time and money for development. But there was no more time or money. A brilliant group of dedicated employees of the Cord Company had turned out an equally brilliant automobile against all odds and for very little money. The engine was an advanced V-8 design, with a Schwitzer-Cummins centrifugal blower that turned at six times engine speed, which topped out at 4,500 rpm, making the blower turn about 27,000 rpm! A friction roller clutch in the blower controlled the inertia force of the blower on rapid acceleration or deceleration and it, too, was a high maintenance item. A soft shear-key in the impeller shaft often broke to prevent damage, but rendered the blower inoperable. Many owners drove the car without realizing the blower wasn't working. The engine produced about 125 horsepower unblown. The centrifugal blower didn't produce a positive boost until the engine exceeded about 2000 rpm, but built boost steadily to the maximum rpm, so it was most effective at fairly high speeds.

The four-speed and reverse transmission was in front of the engine. Shifting was by vacuum and electric circuits with a pre-selector finger ring just below the right side of the steering wheel. Its operation was similar to the Wilson pre-selector on the Talbot Lagos—you put the finger shifter into the gear-slot you wanted, but nothing happened until you depressed the clutch. The Talbot Lagos' Wilson pre-selector box shifted instantly when you depressed the clutch, but on the Cord shifting was slow, especially into low gear, and sometimes nothing happened if everything wasn't operating perfectly. When working properly, it was a very pleasant transmission in the upper three gears, and a big improvement over most manual transmissions of that era. The transmission is the car's worst feature, and another high maintenance item that would have quickly improved if production had continued.

The company published conflicting horsepower ratings that ranged from 170 to 190 hp without any special tuning. The car was good for an honest 110 mph in stock tune. In 1937 that was fast for an American production car. Every 812 Cord left the factory with a guarantee it had been tested in excess of 100 mph. My first Cord had an engraved plate on the dash that read, "This Cord has been tested by Ab Jenkins at 101.5 MPH." How much of this was just sales hype is anybody's guess now.

Without question the thing that has made every 810 and 812 Cord a timeless classic is the body styling by Gordon Buehrig, who said that he was only making fifty dollars a week when he did it. His design made both him and the car famous. The Museum of Modern Art called the 810 and the 812 Cords "Rolling Sculpture."

When Jackie and I were married in 1943, World War II was in full swing and no new cars had been manufactured since 1941. I was working in Los Angeles one day when a shiny black supercharged Cord Phaeton caught my eye in a used car lot. I stopped to look at it. I knew something about Cords because I had owned three Auburns, the Cord's less glamorous relatives. I had seen a few because they were popular in Los Angeles, especially in Hollywood. I thought they were the most gorgeous cars I had ever seen. This one was sort of a puzzle because the paint, chrome and leather were like new, but the black cloth top was in rags and tatters and the engine was in terrible shape. The old Plymouth we were driving for a family car was pretty far gone. I couldn't resist the Cord and bought it for $900.

Even though the Auburn-Cord-Duesenberg Company had gone bankrupt in 1937, the former sales agency in Los Angeles was still in business servicing all those makes in and around Los Angeles. I had the car delivered to the ACD facility where I had them do a complete engine and transmission rebuild. These men were real experts and had complete parts supplies, with some improved parts such as a new hardened low gear that had been a weakness of the Cord. When that was done, I took it to an upholsterer friend in Santa Ana, where we lived, and had a new black convertible top made. It looked and drove like a brand-new automobile, and we loved that car! It attracted a crowd wherever we parked it, and we had to be careful backing up to be sure we wouldn't run over some kid looking under the car. Of course I read all about them in Floyd Clymer's paperback book. They were very low to the ground, and curves and corners could be taken at a much higher speed than with a rear-wheel-drive car so long as you kept applying power. But most of the weight was up front and if you backed off on the throttle in a tight curve, the tail end would break loose. Hard emergency braking could produce the same result as I found out the hard way. On a wet pavement my car once did a complete 360 degrees without leaving my own lane, winding up going in the same direction, with no harm done! It would have been difficult to roll over, however, because of the low center of gravity.

My brother "Brownie" was stationed at Camp Roberts, training draftees, about three hundred miles from Santa Ana. He bought a worn-out Buick Roadmaster convertible sedan to haul as many GIs as he could get in the car to share the cost of driving round trip from Camp Roberts to Santa Ana, to see his wife Katy and his three boys, on a forty-eight hour pass. Feeling sorry for him I temporarily swapped my Cord for his Buick because the Cord was much faster and got better gas mileage. I used his old Buick until the war ended, then I got my Cord back. He drove the Cord flat-out to make the round trip with a few hours to spend with his family. In spite of having been driven hard it never failed him and was still in good condition when I got it back. One day after the war, when I parked it in front of our neon sign plant in Santa Ana, it was stolen. The police found it in an orange grove, but my romance with the Cord was over, and I sold it. Had the ACD Company survived the war, all the car's problems would have been ironed out. I never really forgot that car, that beautiful, shiny, fast convertible, with the chrome exhaust pipes out both sides of the hood, that we drove with the top down in view of the Pacific Ocean, on the highway that the Spanish called El Camino Real (The King's Highway).

It was memories like those that made me determined to buy another Cord. It was an important American Classic, and of all the American cars I would most like to have again it was a 1937 Model 812 Cord Phaeton. I had spent half a lifetime of energy and a lot of money restoring cars that were not much more than junk to begin with. This time I wanted a car that was either a top quality older restoration that was still very good or a good original car that I could have Mark repair or restore. After a lot of searching, I bought my Cord from Ron Starrintino of Long Island, New York. (It seemed that cars I wanted were always very far away.) I had purchased most of my cars sight unseen and did not want to travel to Long Island to see this car. Ron was very honest about the car. He told me its shortcomings—that the car had never been repainted except for fender repair work, that he had put a new top on the car several years before and that the chrome plating on the top bows was in poor shape. Ron was reluctant to sell it without my personal inspection but I got good photographs as well as copies of the history and service documentation and I even wasted $300 to have a professional appraiser inspect the car and give me a written report. Starrintino had owned it for twenty-four years and was only the second registered owner—and the car only had 57,382 original, documented miles! I was not expecting a sixty-year-old car that was never restored to be perfect. It had a great history with a remarkable documented maintenance history, so I bought it, sight unseen, for $80,000. And I was not disappointed when Passport delivered the car to my new shop.

Mr. William H. Patterson brought this new 1937 supercharged Cord Phaeton home to his mansion, where it stayed in the family for the next

The Patterson mansion. The Cord lived here for eighteen years.

eighteen years! His own staff maintained the car, keeping a detailed maintenance record from the first oil change in 1937, with 450 miles on the odometer, to the last oil change at their place in 1955, with 53,006 miles on the odometer. Ron Starrintino provided copies of the original Invoice from Bittorf Motor Company in Baltimore, Maryland, with the net selling price of $2,620 after a $500 cash discount. The date of sale, December 3, 1937, was three months after the factory had closed.

I drove the car quite a bit to discern what all it needed. As particular as I am, I decided it needed too much to do piecemeal. The car would have to be dismantled to paint it properly and to redo all the chrome plating. While the engine ran pretty well and the transmission shifted normally, for a Cord, it had to come out of the car and I decided to rebuild the engine at the same time. Without dismantling the engine its condition was an unknown. In other words, we would do a complete restoration of the car. The only advantage I got by paying top price for a good unrestored car was its provenance. But it had that in spades! This raises a question about buying a car in really bad condition for very little money versus paying top price for a car as good as this one if a restoration is intended. I had usually opted for the former simply because when you begin working on a car that has needs, there is no place to stop. In any event, this time we began with a very good car that had virtually no rust— a most important matter with a Cord, or for any car for that matter. The entire engine and transmission is mounted to a steel subframe that is bolted to a steel beam cross-section built into the monocoque body section. There are stressed, triangulated steel rods that reinforce the attachment of the subframe to the firewall of the body. High-grade steel bolts were used to reinstall these components and a tight fit is critical to prevent shimmy and shake of the front end. The half-shafts of the front drive assembly pass through the holes in the subframe.

As usual, when I decided to buy a Cord, I joined the club. There is an exceptional interest in the Auburn-Cord-Duesenberg automobiles. All of them are recognized as Classics by CCCA and the AACA, and they are always welcome at any club event or car show. They are always popular with the public at Concours d'Élégance events. But beyond their universal acceptance, the ACD Club people are really dedicated to preserving and maintaining these cars, especially the rare Cords and the even more rare and valuable Duesenbergs. I found the club directors and historian to be very helpful and delighted that this car was coming into the club. They had knowledge of the car, but it had not been seen at any club event for many years.

I shipped the engine block, heads and crankcase to Harkins in Watertown to do the machine work. Mark found the centrifugal blower had sheared the half-moon key on the friction-roller clutch shaft, so the blower had not been working when I had driven the car. The shaft had been damaged and bits of metal had scored the aluminum impeller housing. I had SRC Precision Products machine a new shaft, grind the shaft and rollers, heat-treat them and re-bore the blower housing. This cost almost a thousand dollars and it illustrates one of the problems that may be found on the 812 engine even though it may run very well without the blower functioning. The unblown Model 810 produced adequate power to perform comparably to other high quality cars of that era.

In a club bulletin I read how an owner experienced a catastrophic failure of the front splined hubs to which the brake drums are riveted. The original steel plates had first cracked, then disintegrated while he was driving the car. Since ours were off the car I had them magnafluxed and sure enough, my hubs had very fine cracks radiating from each bolthole. These parts are no longer available, so I went looking again. I took them to a welding specialist, an expert who does various types of high-tech welding for the aircraft and space people around Boulder. He machined new high-strength steel plates, cut out the splined hubs from the old plates and welded them together, alternately welding and annealing them in stages. I wrote an article, with photographs, describing exactly how this was done, giving the specifications of the type of steel, welding rod, heat settings and the annealing process, so others who discovered the problem would be able to have the hubs fixed by any competent welder without the research and expense I incurred. This is the sort of help good club people share when they can.

Mark Clayton did his usual perfect paint job on the body parts and carefully assembled the car as all the components that were outsourced came back and were put together. The only thing we did not replace or rebuild was the leather interior. Ron Starrantino had this done a couple of years before I bought it and while it was not quite up to Mark's standards,

The unit body was stripped to bare metal.

The front subframe bolts to the steel cross-beam built into the cowl section.

The beautiful aircraft-influenced instrument panel.

I though it was too good to replace. We had a new black convertible top made. Of course, every bit of chrome plating was redone. The 812 Cord Phaeton has a lot of chrome, and on a black body, it shines like jewelry. Mark had every component that could affect the driving and handling rebuilt, including the leaf springs and the shock absorbers, and also had the engine balanced before it was assembled.

The triangulated steel rods in the engine compartment are very important to prevent cowl-shake and tramping of the front end when driving.

The restored 1936–37 Supercharged Cord Phaeton.

These connections must be kept perfectly tight, with high-strength bolts. Every detail of the engine was correct, including the original air-cleaner. The Cords have one of the most beautiful instrument panels ever designed for an automobile. The full complement of instruments was unusual for American cars in 1936. The radio is to the right and above the switch; the gearshift finger-loop lies just below the wheel.

Jackie and I drove the car to an ACD Club rally in Torrington, Wyoming, that included a side-trip to old Fort Laramie that was so im-

The leather interior was roomy and comfortable, just like the one we had in 1943.

portant for the pioneers heading to California or Oregon. The car was inspected there by Paul Bryant and two club members who then submitted their findings to the club for certification as an original unmodified car as sold by an authorized dealer. This led to a surprise for all. It turned out that the car had been a 1936 un-supercharged Phaeton that had languished in the dealer's inventory. But Mr. Patterson wanted a supercharged phaeton, so the authorized dealer, Bittdorf Motors, took a supercharged engine from a new sedan and installed it in the new 1936 Phaeton. Because the engine swap was done and documented properly by an authorized Cord dealer, the club sanctioned it as a correct, authentic car, but as a 1936, not a 1937! Moreover, the club historian was able to tell me the car had the twenty-ninth phaeton body built. Not the twenty-ninth car, but the twenty-ninth body. I drove the car about 400 miles on this trip, and it was a good opportunity to find all the inevitable bugs that show up after a full restoration. There was good news and bad news, as I told Mark. The car ran cool and the engine was quite strong and would be even better after another thousand miles. I pulled grades up to 7,000 feet in top gear. Both front wheels were throwing grease, perhaps because of being over-greased. The tachometer cable broke, a real inconvenience as I used the tachometer more than the speedometer. The starter Bendix acted up, the brakes needed adjusting and there was too much pedal travel before the brakes operated. Both the brake and clutch pedal springs required too much leg-pressure; lighter springs were needed. The throttle lever that could be used like a "cruise-control," which is nice on a long trip, needed some cable adjustment. The biggest problem was a strong vibration from 60 mph up to about 75, the very range one would use most in modern highway driving. There was a lot of cowl-shake, too. Putting all these problems together, the car was not usable as a tour-car. I sent it back to Mark for more work. Sorting the problems out took several rounds of repairs and road testing. We had the wheels and brakes balanced by a Bear Alignment shop that has the equipment to balance them on the car. The front-end shake and vibration proved to be mostly a matter of re-tightening the subframe and cowl bracing, along with perfect wheel balance.

It took a while but Mark eventually eliminated all the bugs. He tested the car to ninety miles and hour and it ran smoothly, without vibration. I drove the car about 3000 miles before I sold it for $145,000, a little less than my cost, but top price for the best of the Cords. I got great satisfaction from driving a Cord again. It did, indeed, bring Jackie and me fond memories of when the Cord and we were young.

27

The 1939 Alvis Speed 25

On the 4th of July in 1996 Jackie, Jerry, our daughter Robin and I went to the Fort Collins airport to see a B-17 Flying Fortress and a B-24 Liberator, each one of the few remaining examples that were restored and in flying condition. They were there raising money to maintain them, and for a certain fee, people could climb aboard to see the cockpit and the gunner's positions, and for a much larger fee, would be given a short ride. We watched one take off and land and it was fantastic to see and again hear the four engines of those big bombers that had been cranked out by the thousands during World War II.

On a service road that ran parallel to the landing strip I noticed an old low-slung sports car coming pretty fast. It stopped before it reached the crowd, turned around and went back the way it came and out of sight. I only caught a glimpse of it, but I knew it was something interesting. I was pretty sure I knew where it had come from and to whom it belonged. For a short time, after I had sold our first sign plant property in Fort Collins, before Loran Swanson opened his own car shop, I had rented a shop in the small airport complex. Loran had some work done there for my Bugatti. I had briefly met Ray Middleton who owned Q.G. Aviation of America. Ray restored World War II English fighters and light bombers, especially the Spitfires. When you restore planes like those, you're talking *years* and *big* money! Like most British gentlemen, Ray loved old cars. He would pop into our car shop occasionally to see what Loran was working on. I was pretty sure the old sports car had come from Ray's hangar. We drove around there and sure enough, the whole front of the hanger was wide open, and to celebrate the Fourth, they had set chairs and a table out-

Ray Middleton's Alvis Special being serviced by Andrew Sigourney beside a Spitfire.

side, watching the old bombers take off and land right in front of them. They were enjoying some beer and soft drinks and driving the old car, which turned out to be an Avis Speed 20 "Special," meaning that it was modified to suit whatever the owner's wants were. In Ray's case, he wanted it to be a good driver and wasn't too picky about originality. Miles, Ray's 18-year-old son, was having fun driving it up and down the service road. It was the first Alvis I had ever seen in the flesh, so Ray asked Miles to give us rides. He took us, one by one, for a very quick ride up and back on the service road. I was impressed with how well the Alvis ran. Very recently, Ray regaled me with stories of decking the Alvis out in white ribbons, a British custom, for Miles and his bride to use as their "getaway car" when they were married in Minot, South Dakota. Then Ray told about driving the Alvis back from Minot, mostly in the rain, without a top, and because he couldn't see through the spray if anyone was in front of him, he mostly stayed out in front, at 80 miles an hour! Ray said it was fortunate that he kept his flight jacket, helmet and parachute stuffed in the car. They saved him from freezing! Ray is getting ready to put a Speed 25 engine with the 4.3-liter head in his Alvis Special, after which it will be good for another twenty-five years or so. British cars and men are made of good stuff!

It was a great Fourth, but I soon forgot all about Ray's Alvis until the following year when I was deciding what British car I wanted to buy for my little collection. I wanted a car that epitomized the pre-war British sports car: low, rakish, with long swept fenders and those huge P-100 Lucas headlights and horns, and of course it had to have knock-off wire wheels. When I saw the full-color photograph on the back cover of my *Antique Automobile* Vol. 57, No. 2, for March-April 1993, I knew I wanted an Alvis Speed 25, with a Cross & Ellis touring body—preferably this very car. It sported an amateur restoration done by the owner, Don Kolb, and by its looks it appeared to be well done. The article he had written was a blow-by-blow account of buying the car, transporting it, dismantling it and spending nine years of his spare time doing a partial body-off frame-up restoration. The article said that he had a mechanic test the compression and inspect the bottom end of the engine but that they decided it didn't need a rebuild. Don only did the cosmetic detailing of the very handsome engine. The detailed article stated that when the car was finished he and his wife drove it over the course to win First Junior Foreign car at Hershey.

I called Mr. Kolb to see if he was interested in selling the Alvis, only to find that a dealer from England had beat me to it. I got the dealer's name, Plus 4, and phone number. When I called, the dealer said the car had been left with his agent, Wayne Brooks, in Pennsylvania, awaiting shipment to England. I talked to Wayne Brooks, who lived and breathed Alvis automobiles. Wayne was keeping the car until time to ship it and had driven it quite a bit. He gave it very high marks. I thought how unfortunate it was that I had missed buying the car directly from Mr. Kolb because I knew the dealer had paid nothing like the $110,000 he was asking for it. However, by 1997 a complete restoration done by a professional shop in the U.S. would cost as much as the car was worth. I had a week to decide before the car was due to leave for the docks and told the dealer I would think about it. I immediately turned to my car books to bone up on the Alvis.

The Alvis automobile was given birth by T.G. John, an engineer and naval architect who ran a shipyard before the Great War. Then during that war he gained experience building aircraft engines where reliability was job one. That commitment to reliability, which depends on very high quality engineering and manufacturing, was the primary reason Alvis became so highly respected in England. They had built high quality automobiles since the 1920s, deliberately aimed at the upper end of the market, competing with such cars as Bentley. But from the beginning, Alvis cars were of the more sporting type and were quite successful in racing. They were never built in large numbers and for that reason they were less well known in America than the lower priced competitors. But in England their build-quality and performance attracted those with both money and good taste. Alvis built many models and body styles to suit most market demands, but the very best of the pre-war open sports cars were the 3.5 liter and the 4.3 liter Speed 25. Like most high quality English cars, Alvis did not build their own coachwork. Most Speed 25's had very handsome Cross & Ellis bodies, but the best looking, in my view, were the very rare van den Plas Tourers, most often mounted on the 4.3 liter chasis.

The 3.5 and 4.3 liter engines were an all-new six-cylinder unit with a cast iron block and aluminum crankcase. They had a rugged, seven main bearing crankshaft and overhead valves. With three side-draft SU carburetors, coil ignition and dual exhausts the 3.5 liter produced 102 horsepower and could propel the relatively heavy sports car to 95 mph. I say heavy, because the car was built on a very strong steel frame with a heavy cast aluminum firewall that was also a stressed cross-member of the chassis. It had many quality features such as vacuum-assisted brakes, independent front suspension, and a Bijur lubrication system that, by pressing a lever under the dash, sent a small, measured amount of oil to every grease fitting on the car. Bijur is an American company, in Bennington Vermont, that still makes systems for lubricating industrial machines. A reservoir sent oil through small copper pipes to special grease fittings that varied in size to deliver a metered amount of oil for each friction bearing surface that was prone to wear. This lubrication feature on some of the more expensive cars of the pre-war era was party responsible for their longevity. All of my Packards and Pierce Arrows had a Bijur system. The Alvis also had built-in jacks, a Luvax hydraulic shock absorber and ride control that were adjustable from the dashboard. Naturally, it was right-hand drive. Unlike many British companies that bought many parts from vendors, Alvis built everything in their own works. They were the first automobile company in the world to provide a four-speed all synchronized transmission, and it was a pleasure to use, with quick, short, positive throws that were solid as a bank vault. The all leather seats had air bladders instead of springs built into the front cushions and seat backs!

With all these great features, how could I resist? I called Plus 4, haggled the price down to $100,000 and bought it with a wire transfer to their English bank. I had Passport pick the Alvis up at Wayne Brooks' place. The Cross & Ellis four-door open touring body was in excellent shape but

I was surprised when I first attempted to drive it by how difficult it was to get in and out of it. I now weighed about 225 pounds and had mild arthritis in my hips and knees. However, I think a much less rotund person would still have trouble because the width of the front door is very small and even with the seat all the way back, the seat back made the opening even narrower. Once in the car, however, I had enough legroom and I was pretty comfortable. If the top were down I would just open the door, step over the seat, put my left foot on the drive shaft tunnel between the seats and slide down into the bucket seat. If the top was up, it was a real contortion act to get in. Getting out was a bit easier, as I could put my right leg out first, turn in the seat and squeeze out past the steering wheel. Getting into pre-war English cars was never easy for the driver. When I was still pretty slim I bought a 1924 3-liter Red Label Bentley roadster from Paul Hatmon in Independence, Missouri. That Bentley was even worse than the Alvis. Paul delivered it halfway to Hays, Kansas and I was dumb enough to drive that thing from Hays, Kansas, to Fort Collins in the dead of winter! The big steering wheel was right in my chest, the gearshift occupied all the space where my right knee needed to be and the emergency brake lever, which was seriously needed to stop the car, was outside just in front of the door! And later, in Estes Park, I tuned a friend's

Red-Label Speed Model, with all the bells and whistles.

The 1939 Alvis Speed 25 with Cross & Ellis Tourer body, VIN 19575.

The 1924 3-liter Bentley I drove 300 miles in mid-winter!

1929 Phantom II Rolls-Royce. They were the all same. I know that English men are not all midgets! Why didn't the manufacturers provide just a couple more inches for the driver to get in and out? I know that the gentry with enough money to buy a Rolls-Royce simply hired a skinny chauffeur with big arm muscles and a strong right leg and they sat in the back seat.

Only 736 Speed 25's were built including all body styles, of which about 110 are estimated to have survived, and only 14 are known in the United States—so this is a rare car. Sometimes a car can be too rare. Very few people in the U.S. have ever heard of an Alvis, which diminishes its value here. The car was very good in most respects but I was not surprised to find a few things that could have been done better. The rear seat back had been lost, and a new one was made too tall, which made it very conspicuous when the top was down. I shortened it myself. Mr. Kolb had made the carpets personally and they were not perfectly made or fitted. The red lacquer paintwork was very good, but not of show quality. All in all, Mr. Kolb had done a remarkable job on a very complex foreign car.

The beautiful wood dashboard had a full complement of Rolls-Royce quality Smiths instruments that actually worked. Typically for quality English cars of that period, it had a lot of interesting features and gadgets, some of which are amusing in light of modern electronics. For example, the little black lever just under the small instrument to the far right was the spring-loaded turn signal switch. You turn it left to go right or right to go left. It was a clock-works like mechanism that shut off automatically after a few seconds, usually before one got to the corner, so you

The very tight cockpit with the world's first four-speed all synchromesh transmission.

had to turn it again while also turning the steering wheel. It still operated the original turn indicators, the totally useless semaphore type that flipped up those skinny little short arms that were hidden behind the twin spare wheels, so they were impossible for anyone to see. They had tiny little lights so dim you had to strike a match to see if they were burning. I wired around them and added a flasher into the circuit. I also added amber lights on the rear fenders. I wired the little fender-mounted parking lights to use as the front turn signals. For someone approaching in front or in back of me, these provided at least a fighting chance for them to tell that I was probably going to make a turn. Modern electronics were far, far into the future.

The windshield wiper was almost as useless. An electric wire, sheathed in the tiny chrome-plated flexible conduit clipped to the folding windshield, powered the 12-volt motor. The on-off switch was on the hard-to-reach motor itself. And even if you reached it, the wipers moved so slowly they wouldn't keep much rain off the windshield. They would probably be OK for clearing off the perpetual mist in the Scottish moors. But they were still an improvement over the American wipers of that era, which operated by vacuum from the engine manifold. Those stopped completely anytime the engine was pulling very hard.

The six-cylinder Alvis Speed 25 engine with three S.U. carburetors.

The center-mounted dash mirror was equally useless for it was mounted too low to see over the higher rear seat back. So I drilled and tapped the windshield posts to fit a pair of vintage Lucas mirrors outside. And I made the wind-wings. These were all done in the proper vintage style, and were necessary while driving in the U.S. But then, it was all these little idiosyncrasies that made a vintage British sports car so interesting, and with all this, they had real panache. They look like they're doing 100 miles an hour just sitting still. I believe the British of that era would put up with any amount of inconvenience and discomfort as long as they looked good doing it, and in an Alvis Speed 25, they sure looked good!

Once I wedged myself into the Alvis it was a joy to drive. Although the front seats were on adjustable runners, they would not go back far enough because the floor structure that supports the front seats stops short, to allow recessed foot room for the rear seat passenger. I thought to myself that the car would always have a driver but would seldom have back seat passengers, so better they should have occasional cramped foot room than a cramped driver all the time. But then, my strain of the Brookses left England in 1750, so what do I know.

The transmission was a solid piece of work and shifted fast and clean. I would take Jackie for a spin now and then, and of course, the car always drew a lot of questions wherever we parked. It was a good way to provoke conversations. Most convertibles look best with the top down, but I thought this car was equally handsome with the top up. The Alvis has a beautiful front end with the chrome V-shaped radiator shroud and the Crested Eagle radiator cap ornament. The huge, twelve volt P-100 Lucas headlights were surprisingly good, and the horns were tuned with a one-third octave difference between them.

I truly enjoyed that Alvis and drove it quite a bit, especially on our open back roads. One day when I was out for a run on such a road, driving at a pretty good clip, there was a huge jolt and a crash in the engine compartment. I thought I must have hit a big rock. I jammed on the brakes, cut the engine and got out to look under the hood. It was the first and only time I have ever seen what a connecting rod looks like sticking outside the crankcase! A rod had failed and knocked a pretty good-sized hole through the left side of the aluminum crankcase and had also cracked the aluminum on the right side. This was a total surprise because the engine had been running well, and it gave no warning at all. Don Kolb had told me that he had not driven the car much after he finished it. Once he had won first in class at Hershey, his mission was accomplished and he sold the car shortly afterwards. Not rebuilding the engine as he restored the rest of the car left the possibility of just such a catastrophe waiting to happen.

A lady in a car came by, stopped and asked if I had a problem. I explained what had happened and asked if she could drop me off where I could call a tow truck. She took me to her home nearby, and then drove me back to my car after I called. I had the car towed to my home first, to think things over, then after a few calls, I had the car towed to Greeley to my Mercedes mechanic and friend, Tom Troudt, who agreed to pull the engine.

The Alvis factory was still in business but now made only military vehicles and light tanks. I gave some thought to having the engine shipped to England, to Red Triangle, the authorized repair facility and parts source for Alvis cars, which were no longer manufactured. I phoned Red Triangle several times to get estimates of what they would charge to repair the crankcase, or provide a used one and to rebuild the engine and how long it would take. They could not quote a firm price, but it would cost $10,000 or more, plus freight, duty and insurance, and it would take many months. I had noticed that the older I got the more I wanted to get things done quickly. Then I remembered Ray Middleton and his Alvis and went to see what he would advise. Ray surprised me by offering to do the whole engine rebuild at his shop. He was very well qualified since he had built up his own Alvis, and he and his mechanics were, after all, certified aircraft mechanics. So I picked up the engine from Tom and took it to Ray in Fort Collins where he would dismantle it and see what all the problems were, and what new parts I would order from Red Triangle.

When the engine was totally apart, Ray could see that the rod bearing bolts had failed, possibly from metal fatigue or having been over-tightened when the mechanic had examined the bottom end. The rod had come loose and the spinning crankshaft had bent it and knocked it sideways to break the crankcase. Fortunately it had not done much other serious damage.

Ray gave me a list of parts to order from Red Triangle, who took its name from the Alvis badge on the radiator. That list included just about everything except the crankshaft. Ray put one of his best men to repairing the hole and cracks in the crankcase. He used pieces of similar aluminum from an old car or aircraft engine so the metallurgy would be similar, cut them to fit and welded them in. This was a slow, careful job, but after he ground the outside surface and sandblasted the whole aluminum crankcase, you could hardly see where the damage had been. Once we received the new parts from England (at a cost of just under $5,000), Ray assembled the engine himself. We had the crankshaft turned and checked for cracks and straightness in Denver. We sent the head out to have the new valves ground, new guides installed and the head milled. We shipped the repaired crankcase, crankshaft and rods to Harkin Machine shop in Nebraska who cast new babbitt for the main and rod bearings, align bored everything and install new camshaft bearings and fit the new camshaft. When the engine was assembled with the new clutch in place, but without the pan or head, the entire engine and clutch was balanced at the airport. As a suggestion for those who want to restore an engine, it might pay to check the services that are available at any small airport. Aircraft engines are rebuilt to very high standards, and these services are sometimes available for non-aircraft engines as well.

One very important thing that Ray did to this engine was to drill, tap and make up the plumbing for a full-flow oil filter. Like most cars of this era, the Alvis had no oil filter, which may have contributed to its failure. Starting out with a totally clean engine, one may then use modern detergent oil, and with a filter, the engine will stay as clean as a new car's engine. I had the Alvis delivered to Ray's hangar, and he installed the engine. All the accessories, such as the starter, generator, voltage regulator, radiator and carburetors were rebuilt while the engine was being done. When the engine was started and adjusted, you could almost balance a nickel on it while it idled! It really ran very smoothly and was very quiet. Except for the discomfort, I would not have hesitated to drive the car across the whole

The beautiful, low-slung Alvis, better than ever with its rebuilt engine. Good for another 100,000 miles!

United States. That is the value of knowing exactly what has been done to restore a car. I have mentioned "trailer queens" that are only driven enough to put them in and out of the covered trailers to take from one car show to another. If one buys such a car it may be absolutely beautiful in every respect but the engine may not have been touched, mechanically. The Alvis was somewhat like that and the results were dire. To do everything we did to the Alvis engine and its accessories cost $16,635. I sold the car to Bruce Earlin in May of 2000. I took in trade towards the Alvis a very nice restored 1957 S-1 Bentley and a good, unrestored straight eight 1939 Daimler E-4 Sports Saloon. I personally stripped, softened and re-dyed the dry leather interior of the otherwise perfect Bentley and sold it for top price. I also personally did a cosmetic restoration of the Daimler, a car virtually unheard of in the United States. Daimlers have been the choice of British royalty ever since they were built. When I finished the Daimler I advertised it in *Hemmings* and found no takers at a price to cover my cost, so I advertised the car in England and offered to sell it at a loss to get the poor thing back home where it would be loved and cared for. The Daimler was another work of love. I have no idea how I came out financially on this Alvis-Bentley-Daimler thing, nor do I really care. I had a taste of three very fine British cars for a while. I poke fun at their idiosyncrasies but I can't fault their excellent style and build quality.

28

Cars I Admired But Never Owned

To some it may seem that I have owned at least one of every good foreign car ever made, but that is far, far from the truth. There are many that I came close to buying, like a Porsche, for example, but every time I thought about buying a Porsche I would think of something else I would rather have, like another Ferrari. I know the Porsches are wonderful cars. They have to be to have a cult following so dedicated that some owners want to be buried in their cars. But I have never even driven one! I wish I had bought a good 911 Targa that I liked so much, but it's too late, because now I probably couldn't get in one. I would also love to have had an Isotta Fraschini and a Hispano-Suiza if for no other reason than how the beautiful names rolls off the tongue. I especially wanted an Hispano-Suiza. That was the car the World War I flying aces always drove in the movies, with their white scarves streaming in the night air. I came very close to buying a Lagonda several times, and I especially admired the LG-45 that was designed by W.O. Bentley after he sold out to Rolls-Royce and worked for them for a while, then quit because they were not his cup of tea. And speaking of Bentley, I would most certainly like to have owned one of the big 4.5-liter Bentleys of the late 1920s. Just reading about the "Bentley Boys" at Le Mans was enough to turn me into another Walter Mitty, vicariously racing around White House Corner—at night—with one headlight crushed and the other one pointing skyward, and with my front axle bent, but with the iron will to press on, ignoring the pain and blood—and win!

In fact there were a number of British cars I admired because they all had such panache. And some were totally unique, like the early Lanchester. I lusted mightily for a low-chassis 100 Mile an Hour Invicta. That perfect row of rivets down the long hood just made me drool, but our paths crossed only once and I couldn't spare the money. Funny, but I never really wanted a Rolls-Royce because I came up from being poor and I knew I did not belong in a Rolls. For me, it would have been ostentatious to drive one. It would have been like crashing a party. It certainly wasn't because I didn't admire those that were designed by Royce himself. I really wanted a Phantom II Continental very badly, but they were hard to find and always expensive, and I knew I would feel conspicuous in one anyway. I believe that Henry Royce was undoubtedly the most uncompromising perfectionist that the automobile industry ever produced. I could relate to him because he too came up from being poor. Charles Rolls was the marketing man. Their work together created a company that was the pride of England in war and peace. They were both knighted and became Sir Charles and Sir Henry. Did you know that the double-R emblem on a Rolls Royce was originally red—and it was changed to black when Sir Henry died as a symbol of mourning?

There were many other worthwhile Italian cars, like Maserati, built with a passion by six Maserati brothers; Carlo, Bindo, Alfieri, Ernesto, Mario and Ettore. They sound a little like the Marx brothers, but they were dead serious racecar builders and drivers. They began building cars and racing them even before Enzo Ferrari. They never had the winning streak that Ferrari did, usually because of a lack of money, but they often won and they were constantly nipping at the heels of the Bugattis and Ferraris. I especially admired the Birdcage Maserati, the tubular frame of which was like a plate of spaghetti. At one time, Bob Sutherland had the only one in Colorado. Because Ferrari won a lot more often than Maserati did, I'd opt for another Ferrari. There were several models of the Lancia I would love to have, beginning with the Lambda, but the only one I ever had was the little 1.3-liter Fulvia HF, an incredible little car with the lightest, most precise unassisted steering I ever experienced. I could see why they did so well in long-distance rallies.

Oh, and how I would love to have had a Duesenberg when I first became interested in cars and read about them in *Automobile Quarterly*. Having designed a few homes and storefronts I was a firm believer that Frank Lloyd Wright was a genius. I had a small collection of books about him and his work. Can you just imagine how I felt when his *personal* Duesenberg came up for sale after his death? His son-in-law, Wesley Peters, offered it for $10,000, and the original body builder had recently restored it at a cost that exceeded the asking price! Gene Rouse offered to loan me the money to buy it, or to go partners with me, but I couldn't spare the money at the time.

Another car that turned my crank was the Stutz, either the Bearcat or the later double overhead cam DV-32, but it never happened. There were also a number of pre-war French cars I would like to have owned, like the Delahaye and especially a D8 Delage. *Cars of the Connoisseurs* first explained to me what great automobiles they were, but again, I always found something I would rather have—like an 8C-2.3 Alfa Romeo. Oh, well.

29

Conclusion

In the year 2000, I was seventy-eight years old and except for the usual problems of old age I was still in reasonably good health, but I knew the time had come to sell the last of my cars and just remember all the pleasure this off-and-on again hobby gave me for almost forty years since I bought the 1929 Chrysler roadster. I believe my experience was rather unusual because I had that small spark of artistic taste and creativity that made me home in on some of the best and most beautiful cars the world had to offer in their times. There have been and are still many fine car collections. At one time Bill Harrah's collection held over 1,100 restored and un-restored cars. The Nethercutt Classic automobile collection is one of the finest ever, and is endowed to perpetuate its care. But most of these collections are static. The best collection, in my experience, was Briggs Cunningham's, consisting mostly of cars he had owned and driven, then "put out to pasture" in his museum. Those cars were started and allowed to run once a week, and were *driven* around their big parking lot once a month enough to warm them up to operating temperatures to keep them in perfect working order. Many of Cunningham's cars went to the Collier Collection in Florida where I'm sure the Colliers see that they are still driven.

It was unique that I, just an ordinary guy, bought each car and restored it to drive for a while in order to experience firsthand what they were like. I got to know their mechanical components intimately, and to read about them and to appreciate the designers, engineers and craftsmen who built them. I don't believe there have been many ordinary men who had the experience that I had owning and driving so many cars that are now almost priceless. Also, this hobby put me in touch by correspondence, by phone conversations and in person with hundreds of very interesting people all over the world.

Even though they were mine only briefly, at today's prices I owned somewhere between thirty and forty million dollars' worth of cars. Many people have asked me if it doesn't "just make me sick" to have sold those cars for so little, knowing what they're worth now. My answer is always the same, "No, it doesn't, because that was all they were worth when I sold them." That's not to say I don't wish I had held on to one or two of them. I couldn't afford a collection, but I certainly could have afforded a couple, or maybe just the 2.9 Alfa that is now worth around ten million dollars. Cars of that type and from that era have outperformed the stock market by a huge margin, but I don't think they're likely to have such huge appreciation in the future. Many collector cars can be purchased today that are fun to drive and are also good investments, that will almost guarantee your money back, with interest, when you want or need to sell them. But the ones I loved are masterpieces, like a fine old masterpiece painting. There were never very many, never enough to meet the demand, and thus the prices go up.

The author, with no regrets.

I have come to realize that no one really "owns" such cars. We are merely the stewards entrusted with their care and maintenance. The cars I loved so much are now mostly in the hands of very wealthy people, which is probably a good thing, for just to maintain the cars and to make such new parts as may be necessary to keep them running is very expensive.

I have no idea whether I made or lost money in the final analysis. I kept good records of each car for tax purposes but I did not keep a running account. I didn't want it to be a business, but neither did I want to lose money. The dollars I made on cars in the first ten or fifteen years were worth much more than the dollars I lost in later years because of inflation. If I only broke even, what other great hobby could I have had that cost nothing?

I wonder at what point cars may have or will become too difficult or too costly to restore like we restored the Classics. Certainly, computerization of the automobile has made a profound difference in the cars we drive today. They are not as distinctive but they are better, faster, safer, more efficient, and infinitely more comfortable. But they don't thrill me like my 8C-2.3 Alfas or my 250 MM Ferraris did.

It's been a wonderful ride!

Index

DATE DUE
